GW01003177

CUBE
BOOK

HORSES

WHITE STAR PUBLISHERS

TEXTS BY

GABRIELE BOISELLE

HENRY DALLAL

ATTILA KORBELY

PAOLO MANILI

SENIO SENSI

MEDFORD TAYLOR

**project manager
and editorial director**
VALERIA MANFERTO DE FABIANIS

graphic design
CLARA ZANOTTI

graphic layout
MARIA CUCCHI

editorial staff
GIADA FRANCIA
ENRICO LAVAGNO
ALBERTO BERTOLAZZI

translation
TIMOTHY STROUD

© 2005 WHITE STAR S.P.A.
VIA CANDIDO SASSONE, 22-24
13100 VERCELLI - ITALY
WWW.WHITESTAR.IT

REVISED EDITION 2007

ISBN 978-88-544-0253-9

REPRINTS:
1 2 3 4 5 6 11 10 09 08 07

Printed in China
Color separation: Chiaroscuro, Turin

CONTENTS
HORSES

1 ● Great Britain. The graceful profile of an Arabian.

2-3 ● France. The semi-wild horses of the Camargue.

4-5 ● USA. A herd of horses in the Southwest.

6-7 ● Italy. Pure competition at the Palio in Siena!

9 ● USA. This bay is distinguished by the white heart standing out on its forehead.

11 ● The Netherlands. Friesians boast proud and wavy manes.

12-13 ● USA. An Appaloosa with a leopard coat.

14-15 ● Austria. A Haflinger pony galloping.

16-17 ● Argentina. A *gaucho* and Criollos on the pampa.

Introduction

by Paolo Manili

Over the millennia the horse has exercised an immense influence over the development of humanity; civilization would have evolved differently had the creature not existed. It was in earliest prehistory that man transformed the horse from a tasty prey into a means of transport, working tool and war machine. In addition, by arousing passions and ambition in man, the horse gave rise to great deeds, encouraged human migrations and conquests, and determined human events and destinies. The horse has also inspired countless generations of painters and sculptors, poets and

● Iceland. A wavy mane frames the gentle gaze of an Iceland pony, a docile,
affectionate and reliable animal.

Introduction

MUSICIANS, WHOSE REPRESENTATIONS OF THE HORSE'S FORM, PER-
FORMANCE AND NATURE HAVE REFLECTED THE TENDENCIES OF EVERY
CIVILIZATION AND CULTURE THROUGHOUT HISTORY. IN MYTHOLOGY,
THE HORSE WAS FUSED WITH MAN TO FORM THE CENTAUR; IT WAS GIV-
EN WINGS TO BECOME A HIPPOGRIFF; IN REALITY, THE SPECIES ADAPT-
ED TO EVERY CLIMATE AND ENVIRONMENT AND BECAME DEEPLY
ROOTED IN HUMAN CUSTOMS AND BEHAVIOR. THE WAYS IN WHICH THE
HORSE CONTINUES TO INFLUENCE OUR WAY OF LIVING, SPEAKING,
DRESSING, THINKING AND DREAMING ARE NUMBERLESS AND BEAR
WITNESS TO THE TIMES IN WHICH MAN AND HORSE COULD NOT DO
WITHOUT EACH OTHER. WHERE MAN CONDITIONED THE NATURE OF HIS
FOUR-LEGGED FRIEND BY CREATING DIFFERENT BREEDS, EACH SUITED

Introduction

TO A PARTICULAR PURPOSE (DRAUGHT, PACK, SADDLE AND RACE HORSES), THE HORSE CONTINUED TO INFLUENCE THE MODUS VIVENDI OF HIS MASTER-CUM-FRIEND. IN MORE RECENT TIMES, VEHICLES HAVE LARGELY REPLACED HORSES IN THEIR DAILY TASKS, YET, FOLLOWING A MASSIVE BUT BRIEF DECLINE IN THEIR PHYSICAL PRESENCE, THEY HAVE BEEN RETURNED TO FASHION THROUGH A GROWING ENVIRONMENTAL AND ANIMALIST AWARENESS THAT HAS RESULTED IN THEIR ESTABLISH-ING THEMSELVES AS POPULAR RECREATIONAL COMPANIONS. THUS THEY STILL RACE ON FAMOUS COURSES, COMPETE AT THE OLYMPICS, POPULATE FARMS AND THE COUNTRYSIDE, AND ALLOW TOURISTS AND OTHERS TO ENJOY THE BEAUTY OF NATURE FROM A SADDLE. THERE IS AN ENGLISH SAYING 'THERE ARE TWO TYPES OF PEOPLE: HORSE RID-

Introduction

ERS AND NEUROTICS,' THUS SUMMING UP THE MODERN RELATIONSHIP

BETWEEN MAN AND HIS MOUNT, ONE THAT GOES BEYOND PSYCHOLO-

GY. AND THIS RELATIONSHIP HAS BEEN TAKEN FURTHER TO INCLUDE

RIDING THERAPY, IN WHICH THE HANDICAPPED BENEFIT FROM A RELA-

TIONSHIP WITH A HORSE. THE SPLENDID PHOTOGRAPHS IN THIS BOOK

ILLUSTRATE THE THREE THOUSAND YEARS OF THE HORSE WORLD ON

PLANET EARTH. IT IS A WELL-MERITED TRIBUTE TO OUR COMPANION –

WHO HAS WORKED FOR US, FOUGHT FOR US AND PATIENTLY TRANS-

PORTED US.

23 ● France. A powerful and very arched neck gives the Arabian horse a very noble appearance.

24-25 ● Great Britain. A cavalry regiment on parade in one of London's streets.

26-27 ● Austria. A Lipizzaner from Vienna's Spanish Riding School performs perfect acrobatics.

28-29 ● Barbados. A Thoroughbred is first across the line in a this race.

BREEDS and their CHARACTERISTICS

GABRIELE BOISELLE

• France. A splendid Arabian sorrel.

INTRODUCTION Breeds and their Characteristics

Some breeds just tug at one's heart, but above all others the Arabians do. Charming, beautiful, intelligent and playful, they are eager to connect with people; they are curious about everything new and try to please their humans, whom they believe to be their own. Then there are Friesian horses, absolutely gentle and humble with those who work with them day by day. But the moment they are free, they fly over the earth, no longer earthbound, with their floating manes and 'feathers' around their legs and their huge tails which seem to be created of waves of black

● Portugal. A white Lusitanian plays in Mediterranean waves.

INTRODUCTION Breeds and their Characteristics

HAIR. THEY WERE BRED TO IMPRESS IN FRONT OF THE SPECIAL

FRIESIAN SJEEß WITH THEIR EXTENDED TROT. BUT WHILE THEY ARE

GREAT DRESSAGE HORSES THEY ARE ALSO IDEAL FOR CIRCUS WORK.

NO HORSE SHOW CAN EXPECT TO SUCCEED WITHOUT THE PER-

FORMANCE OF FRIESIAN HORSES. THEIR CLOSE RELATIVES, THE AN-

DALUSIANS, WHICH ARE MOSTLY GREY HORSES WITH FLOATING

MANES, CAN BE ADMIRED AS WELL IN THE DIFFERENT DISCIPLINE OF

HIGH-STYLE DRESSAGE. CENTURIES AGO THEY WERE BRED TO PER-

FORM THE CAPRIOLE AND PESADE AS USEFUL FIGHTING STRATEGIES

IN BATTLE. LATER ON, HORSEMANSHIP BECAME AN ART AND TODAY

THE LIPIZZANER HORSES PERFORM THESE FIGURES IN THE SPANISH

INTRODUCTION Breeds and their Characteristics

RIDING SCHOOL IN VIENNA. ALL OVER EUROPE THERE ARE DIFFERENT

BREEDS OF HORSES DESCENDED FROM FOREBEARS BRED FOR SPE-

CIAL MILITARY NEEDS: CAVALRY HORSES FOR WAR; HORSES EASY TO

RIDE; AND FAST HORSES ABLE TO JUMP OVER OBSTACLE. THEN

THERE ARE THE WORKING HORSES; HEAVY BREEDS FOR PULLING

WAGONS, TRANSPORTING GOODS, AND FOR PLOWING FIELDS. ON

SUCH HORSES' SHOULDERS LAYING THE RESPONSIBILITY FOR AGRI-

CULTURAL LIFE. IN THEIR MILLIONS THEY BROUGHT IN THE HARVEST

AND ASSURED WEALTH AND PROSPERITY. SADLY, WITH THE ADOPTION

OF INDUSTRIAL MACHINERY MOST OF THEM WERE NO LONGER NEED-

ED AND WERE SLAUGHTERED. ONLY A DECADE AGO DID PEOPLE BE-

INTRODUCTION Breeds and their Characteristics

GIN TO UNDERSTAND THAT THEY HAD TO PRESERVE THESE OLD

BREEDS IN RECOGNITION OF ALL THE WORK THEIR ANCESTORS HAD

DONE. AS A RESULT, THERE IS NOW A RENAISSANCE IN THE BREEDING

OF DRAFT HORSES IN EUROPE AND AMERICA. OLD BREEDS LIKE THE

ARDENNER, PERCHERON, NORIKER, BRETONE, COB NORMAND,

SHIREHORSE, CLYDESDALES AND OTHERS ARE BECOMING KNOWN

AGAIN, HORSE LOVERS VERY OFTEN UNDERESTIMATE THE VALUE OF

PONY BREEDS. THEY ARE SEEN AS KIDS' HORSES, NOT TO BE TAKEN

SERIOUSLY. BUT NOW, WHEN THE PRICE OF A 'SPORT' PONY CAN EAS-

ILY BE TRIPLE THE PRICE OF A REASONABLY ACCOMPLISHED SHOW

HORSE, PEOPLE ARE HAVE BECOME AWARE OF THE POTENTIAL VAL-

INTRODUCTION Breeds and their Characteristics

UE OF THE "SMALL ONES." IN FACT, OVER HISTORY, PONIES HAVE BEEN

USED IN AGRICULTURAL WORK AND IN PULLING WAGONS, JUST LIKE

DRAUGHT HORSES. FOR EXAMPLE, IN NORWAY, THE FJORD PONY

FROM WAS USED ON THE VERY STEEP HILLS ALONG THE FJORDS,

WHERE BIGGER HORSES HAD TOO LITTLE ROOM TO WORK SUCCESS-

FULLY. IN IRELAND, THE CONNEMARA PONY WAS ONCE A REAL WORK-

ING BREED THAT PULLED CARTS. ONLY ON THE WEEKENDS DID THE

FARMERS RACE THEM AGAINST EACH OTHER. TODAY THE CON-

NEMARAS PRODUCE SUPERCLASS JUMPING PONIES FOR INTERNA-

TIONAL COMPETITIONS. FOR CENTURIES EVERY COUNTRY BRED THE

HORSES IT NEEDED. THE BLOODLINES OF MOST BREEDS HAVE BEEN

Breeds and their Characteristics
Introduction

IMPROVED BY ENGLISH THOROUGHBREDS AND BY ARABIANS. BUT
THE ACTUAL DIVERSITY OF THE BREEDS RESULTS FROM THE SELEC-
TIVE BREEDING DIFFERENT BREEDERS HAVE UNDERTAKEN. IN THE FU-
TURE, WE WILL HAVE DEMANDS FOR HIGH-QUALITY STOCK, AND
HIGH-INTENSITY DEMANDS AND PEOPLE WILL ALSO BREED THE
HORSE MOST SUITABLE FOR COMPETITION AND FOR RECREATIONAL
RIDING, EITHER BASED ON THE WESTERN OR ON THE ENGLISH RIDING
SYSTEM. AND FINALLY, THERE IS ONE VERY IMPORTANT REASON TO
BREED HORSES, NOW THAT WE NO LONGER NEED THEM TO ENSURE
OUR DAILY SURVIVAL – THE LOVE WE FEEL FOR THEM IN GETTING TO
KNOW THEM.

● Iceland. Rustic and tough, the Iceland has a thick mane.

The Netherlands. Detail of a Friesian's raven-black, finely curled mane.

42 ● The Netherlands. The Friesian's legs are not very long and the hocks are rather hairy.

43 ● The Netherlands. A black Friesian plays in the rain.

The Netherlands. With their "curly" manes, Friesian horses boast unique elegance.

The Netherlands.
Friesian at the gallop in the
Dutch countryside.

48 ● The Netherlands. Docile and intelligent, Andalusians are excellent dressage horses.

49 ● The Netherlands. A bridled Andalusian during a horse show.

● Portugal. The docile and brave Lusitano is a very rare horse. It is estimated that there are only 20,000 or so around the world.

● Germany. The coats of Arabian horses vary in color, often with white splotches on the legs and head.

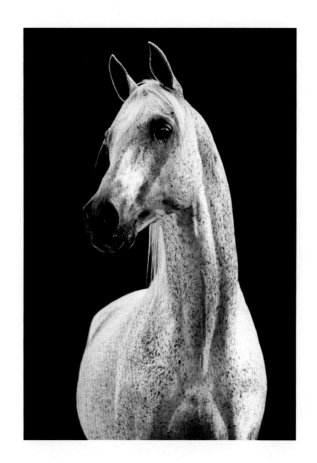

54 ● Germany. Excellent riding horses, Arabians are quite frisky.

55 ● Germany. A fine Arabian thoroughbred seems to pose proudly for the camera.

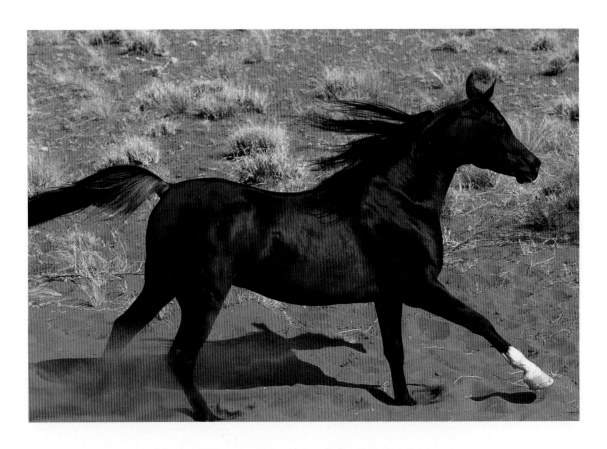

56 ● USA. Among Arabian horses, black ones with white hocks are the rarest and most sought after.

57 ● USA. Arabians are slender in build and of a nervous disposition.

58-59 ● Spain. Traditionally used for riding, Arabians seem born to gallop.

60 and 61 ● France. The sturdy head of a Comtois reveals its docile but willing nature.

62-63 ● France. The Comtois, a French draught horse, in the Middle Ages they were used as warhorses.

● Iceland. The Iceland pony can ridden, but it can serve as a packhorse or draft animal. Moreover, it does not need to be stabled during the winter.

66 • Iceland. With its intelligent
eye and fringed mane, Iceland
ponies win sympathy at first glance.

66-67 • Iceland. The Iceland
breed was created at the start of
the 20th century by crossing local
ponies with ponies that
Norwegians brought to the islands.

● Iceland. Seen here at the gallop in the snow, the Iceland is used as a saddle pony for inexpert riders.

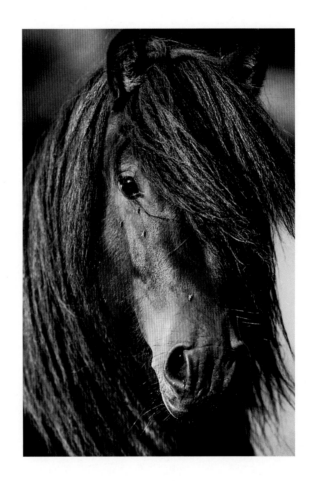

● Great Britain. A long-established English breed from the Devon moors,
the Dartmoor is strong and tireless.

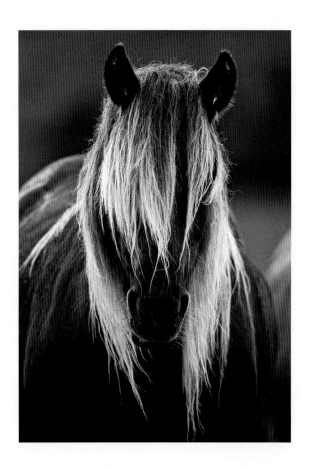

Great Bretain. Though sturdy and unflagging, the long blond manes
of Shetland ponies make them seem cuddly.

● Great Britain.
Shetland ponies,
originally from the
Scottish mainland, in
particular from the
Orkneys and Isle of
Shetland, were originally
used as draught animals
in mines and agriculture.

76-77 ● Argentina. This close-up of a Criollo shows its tenacious and willing spirit.

77 and 78-79 ● Argentina. A saddle horse, the Criollo was derived from crossing Arabian, Berber and Andalusian horses brought to South America by the Spanish.

80-81 ● Argentina. The Criollo is the horse used by the *gauchos* of Latin America: they are sturdy, quick and agile in working with cattle.

82-83 ● Argentina. A Criollo's coat may be any of several shades, but is often marked with white and "mule lines."

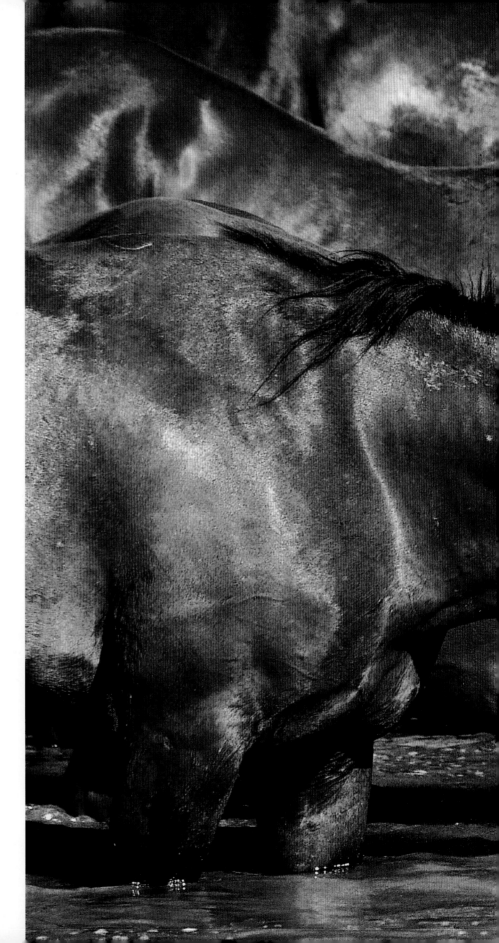

84-85 ● Italy. Balanced and strong, and a good jumper, the Maremmano is generally bay.

86-87 ● Italy. Originally short, strong and skittish, through crosses with English breeds the Maremmano has become the elegant and classic military horse of today.

Ireland. The Gypsy Vanner is not really a breed but a horse of changeable appearance.

● Ireland. A saddle horse used by the military, and originally from Ireland,
the Gipsy Vanner is currently used in equestrian tourism.

Ireland. The Gipsy Vanner is tough and dynamic: here we see their elegance, thick mane, long tail and hairy hocks.

Ireland. Bred with
black, bay, gray and
sorrel coats, Gipsy
Vanners are also
attractive piebald.

96-97 ● Austria. The Haflinger is originally from the Tyrol and therefore is strong and tough, fully suited to the alpine environment.

98-99 ● Austria. The Haflinger is considered a pony by experts due to its short, sturdy legs.

100 and 101 ● Austria. This tyrolean pony's gentle expression belies a good
and intelligent nature.

102-103 ● Austria. With their hooves hidden in the fresh snow, this Haflingers seems
perfectly at home on the mountain slopes.

104-105 and 105 ● Austria. A herd of Haflingers rises to a gallop on a snowy meadow in the Tyrol.

106-107 ● USA. The Pinto was first bred by Native Americans looking for "colored" wild horses to cross with horses of Spanish origin.

108 ● USA. The Pinto Arab's graceful action, especially at the gallop, is the breed's most sought-after characteristic.

109 ● USA. This Pinto Arab filly displays all the typical gracefulness and elegance of her breed.

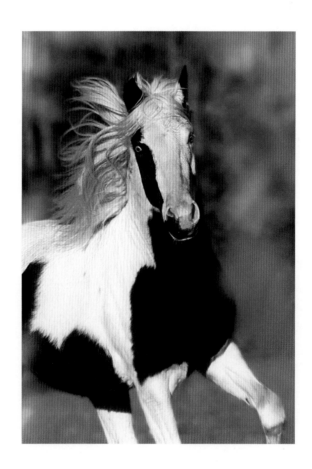

USA. The Comanches were the first to begin selection of the Pinto,
and ended up with the piebald we know.

" **A** LINEAGE AS NUMEROUS AND NOBLE AS THAT OF THE HORSE NATURALLY BOASTS GREAT "FAMILIES." THESE FAMILIES, COMMONLY KNOWN AS BREEDS, HAVE BEEN SHAPED BY MAN THROUGH THOUSANDS OF YEARS OF PATIENT WORK, AND HAVE CREATED THE MOST FORMIDABLE ALLIANCE EVER FORGED IN NATURE BETWEEN SUCH DIVERSE BEINGS. "

● USA. Tough and characteristic in appearance, the Pinto has always been used to work with herds and in rodeos.

114 ● Germany. Manes flying in the wind, three Irish Tinkers break into a gallop.

115 ● Germany. The magnificent Irish Tinker is descended from horses selected by nomadic tinkers in Ireland.

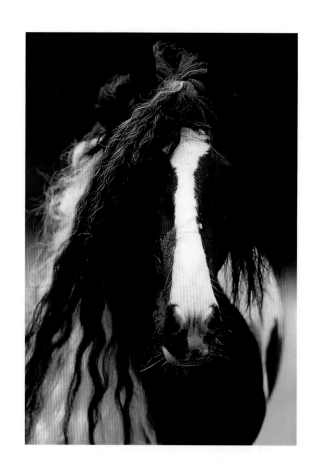

● Germany. Besides a dark complexion, Irish Tinker have spectacular long hair.

Germany. Because of its "square" structure, the Irish Tinker is an excellent workhorse, but it also has a docile and sensitive temperament.

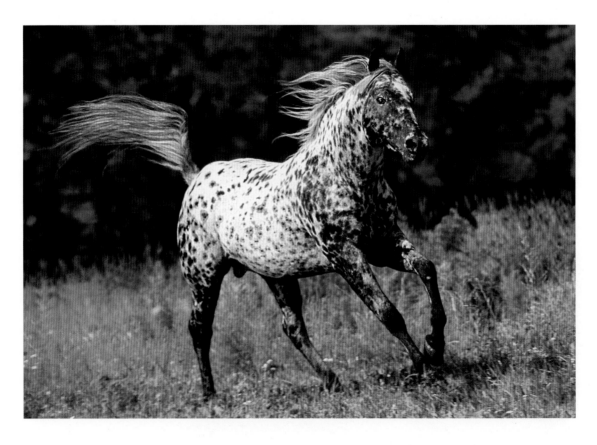

120 ● USA. The Appaloosa is the classic "Western" horse, ideal for galloping, with plenty of speed and stamina. This type of coast is described as "marble."

121 ● USA. The Appaloosa's speckled coat gives this sturdy, vigorous and muscular horse a gentle complexion.

"AMONG HORSES, THE INFINITE COMBINATIONS OF COLORS AND PATTERNS OF THEIR COATS REFLECT FAR MORE THAN MERE AESTHETIC SURFACE TRAITS. THIS IS BECAUSE THEY IDENTIFY NOT ONLY A BREED OF HORSES BUT A DISTINCT PERSONALITY. REGARDLESS OF WHETHER IT IS AN ARABIAN OR NORMAN, FRIESIAN OR APPALOOSA, THE HORSE IS AN INDIVIDUAL FIRST AND FOREMOST, WITH ITS OWN PERSONALITY AMONG THE OTHERS."

122 and 123 ● USA. The unique pattern on an Appaloosa's coat is a sort of identity card that makes it immediately identifiable.

124-125 ● Great Britain. Shire horses have distinctive long hair around their hocks.

126 • Great Britain. Though taller, Shires resemble Friesians, a breed with which they were probably crossed in the Middle Ages.

127 • Great Britain. Dark-haired Shire horses (whether black or bay) often have white patches.

128 ● USA. The Morgan horse, seen here with a palomino coat, is an excellent trotter.

129 ● USA. A horse from the American "frontier" like the Appaloosa, the Morgan is extremely versatile, and can be ridden or used as a draft animal. It is also ideal for competitions and parades.

● Great Britain. Two Shires at the gallop shine with sweat; note their huge and powerful muscles.

USA. Though particularly sensitive to sunlight, the American White is very vigorous and versatile. Muscular, with a broad chest and strong legs, American Whites have the characteristics of the breed's ancestor, Old King, who lived in the early 1900s.

134 ● Great Britain. The Thoroughbred is a graceful and nimble horse made for galloping.

135 ● Great Britain. An English Thoroughbred has an elegant, lean head.

HORSES in the WILD

ATTILA KORBELY

INTRODUCTION Horses in the Wild

As far as looks go, horses display a stunning range of variation. Consider just a few examples: Shetland and Fjord ponies reminiscent of Disney cartoons; Friesian horses boasting majestic manes; massive draft horses; graceful Thoroughbreds; wild Mustangs – and the list could go on. But this was not always the case. The ancient horse hails from North America. Before vanishing from that continent, however, some horses crossed the Bering Strait and migrated to Asia, subsequently populating all of Eurasia. Humans began domesticating the horse approximately 5000 years ago, when the ancient horse probably ex-

INTRODUCTION Horses in the Wild

HIBITED A LIMITED RANGE OF VARIATION IN SHAPE AND COAT COLOR,

DEPENDING ON HOW THE ANIMAL HAD ADJUSTED TO ITS HABITAT. TO-

DAY'S DIVERSITY IN SHAPE, COLOR AND SIZE IS LARGELY DUE TO HU-

MAN INTERVENTION. THIS MAKES IT CLEAR WHY WE SHOULD NOT RE-

GARD FERAL HORSES – WHOSE ANCESTORS HAD BEEN DOMESTIC

HORSES – AS WILD HORSES. FORTUNATELY, THE ANCESTOR OF TO-

DAY'S HORSES, THE ASIATIC WILD HORSE, SURVIVES IN A SINGLE POP-

ULATION THAT LIVES ON THE STEPPES OF DZUNGARIA. AT THE END OF

THE 1960S, THIS POPULATION BECAME EXTINCT. FORTUNATELY, BY

THEN A FEW SPECIMENS WERE IN EUROPEAN ZOOS. EVENTUALLY, 11

ANIMALS WERE SELECTED FOR BREEDING, AND DUE TO AN INTERNA-

INTRODUCTION Horses in the Wild

TIONAL PROGRAM THE NUMBER OF WILD HORSES WAS BROUGHT

BACK TO OVER 1500. THIS WAY, THE ASIATIC WILD HORSE (THE ONLY

TRUE WILD HORSE SUBSPECIES TO SURVIVE) COULD BE RETURNED TO

ITS ORIGINAL HABITAT. THESE HORSES GO BY SEVERAL NAMES – THEY

ARE VARIOUSLY CALLED PRZEWALSKI'S HORSE (NAMED AFTER THE

RUSSIAN EXPLORER-NATURALIST WHO DISCOVERED THEM IN 1879),

TAKHI (THEIR MONGOLIAN NAME) AS WELL AS ASIATIC OR MONGOLIAN

WILD HORSE. THE ASIATIC WILD HORSE HAS A DISTINCTIVE APPEAR-

ANCE – IT IS ZEBRA-LIKE IN ITS MOVEMENT AS WELL AS APPEARANCE.

BUT WHAT EXACTLY ARE THE DIFFERENCES BETWEEN ASIATIC WILD

HORSES AND HORSES THAT WERE ONCE DOMESTICATED AND ARE

NOW FERAL? FIRST, WILD HORSES COME FROM ANCESTORS THAT

INTRODUCTION Horses in the Wild

HAVE NEVER BEEN DOMESTICATED. THEIR 'WILDNESS' IS DEFINED BY

ANOTHER IMPORTANT ASPECT. HUMANS USUALLY HERD HORSES

WITH THE HELP OF A DOG OR A WHIP DOG, BUT A WILD HORSE CAN

ONLY BE HERDED BY OTHER WILD HORSES. WHEN A STALLION WITH A

HAREM APPROACHES ANOTHER, HE HERDS HIS MARES AND FOALS

WITH NECK AND HEAD HELD STIFFLY AHEAD, EARS FLATTENED. BUT

THESE CHARACTERISTICALLY STUBBORN ANIMALS DO NOT TEND TO

LIKE THIS KIND OF DISPLAY, AND THE HERD TRIES TO KEEP THE IN-

TRUDING STALLION AT BAY BY BITING AND KICKING. HOLDING TO-

GETHER A LARGE HAREM TAKES VIGILANCE, PERSISTENCE AND ENER-

GY. ASIATIC WILD HORSES LIVE IN SOCIAL GROUPS OR SOMETIMES

SOLITARILY. UNLIKE DOMESTICATED AND FERAL HORSES, THEY ARE EX-

INTRODUCTION Horses in the Wild

TREMELY AGGRESSIVE; A STALLION NOT ONLY PROTECTS ITS HAREM

AND FOALS BUT SOMETIMES CONFRONTS OTHER HORSES FROM

MILES AWAY TO FEND THEM OFF. THE WIND BRINGS A SHORT NEIGH

ACROSS THE STEPPE. THE DOMINANT MALE LEAVES HIS HAREM AND

CANTERS A FEW HUNDRED YARDS TOWARD THE SOURCE OF THE

SOUND AND THEN STANDS STILL AND LISTENS WHILE FIXING HIS GAZE

ON A SINGLE SPOT ON THE HORIZON. HIS HAREM GATHERS AROUND

HIM, LOOKING WORRIED. IF NEITHER OF THE MALES BACKS OFF, THEN

BOTH BEGIN FIERCELY TOSSING THEIR HEADS BACK AND FORTH,

STAMPING ON THE GROUND WITH THEIR FRONT FEET, NEIGHING AND

CALLING ON THE OTHER TO LEAVE. THEN, AS THOUGH THEY WERE

PERFORMING AT A SPANISH RIDING SCHOOL, THEY BEGIN A COLLECT-

Horses in the Wild
Introduction

ED TROT TOWARD EACH OTHER ARCHING THEIR NECKS, EVENTUALLY JUMPING AT THE OTHER. THIS GESTURE IS JUST A SIMPLE SHOW OF POWER. WHEN THE STAKES ARE HIGHER, HOWEVER, AND A STALLION IS TRYING TO ACQUIRE A HAREM, THERE CAN BE BLOODSHED, SOME-TIMES ENDING WITH THE DEATH OF ONE OF THE CONTENDERS. WILD HORSES HAVE A STRIKINGLY SWEET HABIT OF GROOMING: THEY STAND LANGUIDLY IN PAIRS, FACE TO FACE, FOR HOURS ON END, PECKING AND NIPPING AT EACH OTHER'S NECKS AND SIDES. DURING THIS "TEAM-BUILDING EXERCISE," AN AURA OF SERENITY DESCENDS OVER THE ANIMALS, MOMENTARILY OBSCURING THEIR WILD NATURE. . . .

145 ● France. A horse in the Camargue dashes across a ford in the Rhone delta.

146-147 ● France. The Rhone's chilly waters don't deter this playful herd.

France.
Since most of the herds
of horses of the
Camargue roam freely,
they must move often to
find food in the poor
lands of the marshes of
the Rhone Delta.

France. The horses of the Camargue, which are mainly gray in color, live semi-wild in the unique environment of the marshlands, to which they have adapted perfectly.

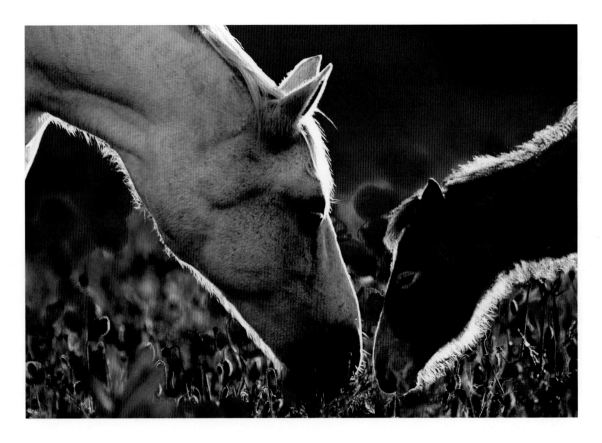

152 and 153 ● France. Camargue horses graze amid the corn poppies of the French Midi.

154-155 ● Portugal. Horses are free to gallop unimpeded on the plains of Portugal.

156-157 ● USA. North Americas open spaces seem ideal for wild horses.

● Iceland. Originally selected as mountain horses, Iceland ponies are completely at ease on rough terrain and have no trouble climbing the steepest slopes.

● Iceland. Ponies in Iceland have an extra gait known as *tølt*; it consists of bringing both legs on one side forward at the same time.

● Iceland. The moors and grasslands on Iceland's hills are home to half-wild herds of horses.

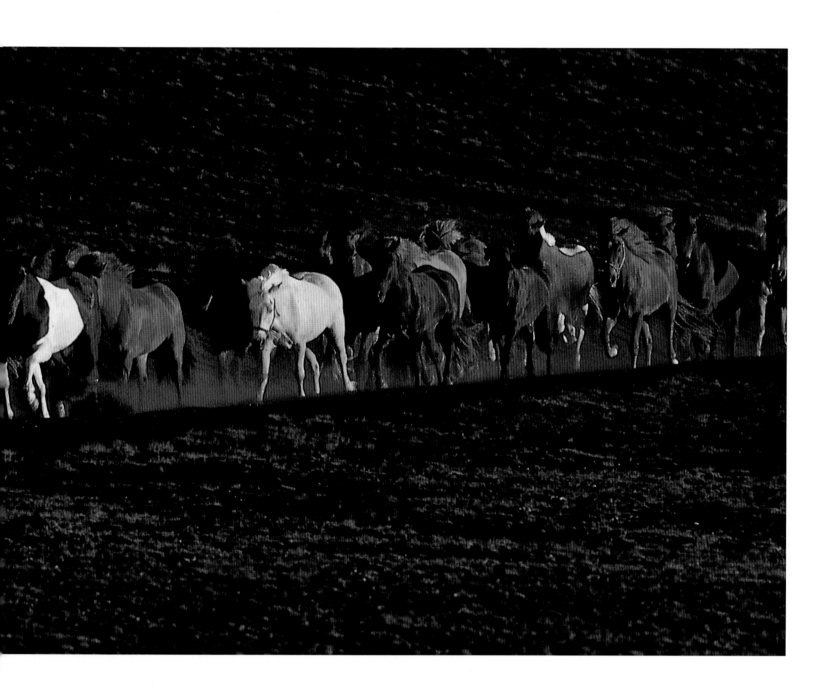

● Iceland. A line of ponies heads down a path in Iceland using the *tølt* gait.

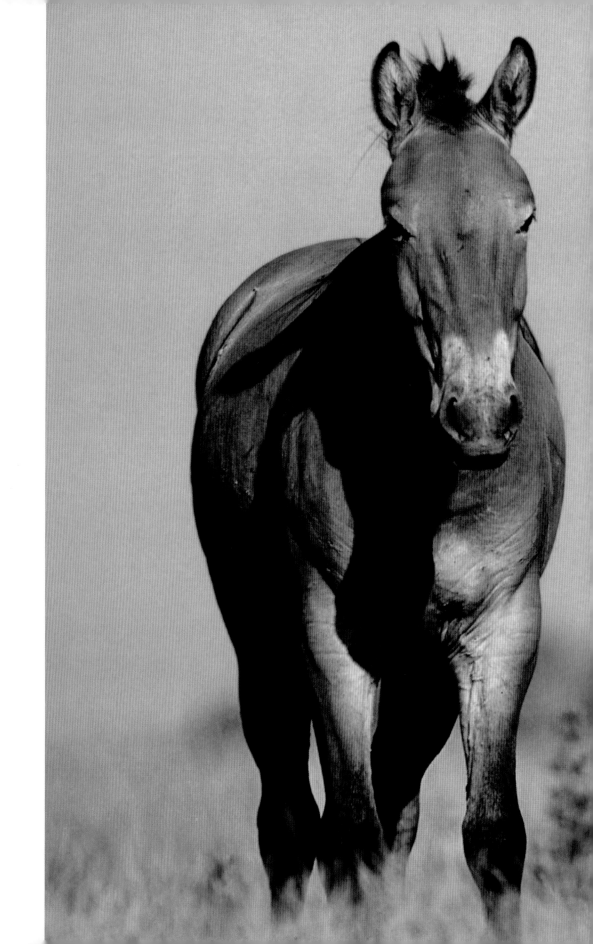

166-167 ● Russia. Originally from Mongolia, Przewalsky horses are also known as wild Asian horses, though now they have almost disappeared from the Mongolian prairies.

168-169 ● Argentina. The permanently snow-covered Patagonian Andes provide an impressive backdrop for this cavalcade.

170-171 ● USA. A group of twenty or twenty-five mustangs at the gallop during a North American winter.

● Great Britain. Born virtually immune to the cold, these ponies seem to enjoy themselves on the snowy slopes of Scotland.

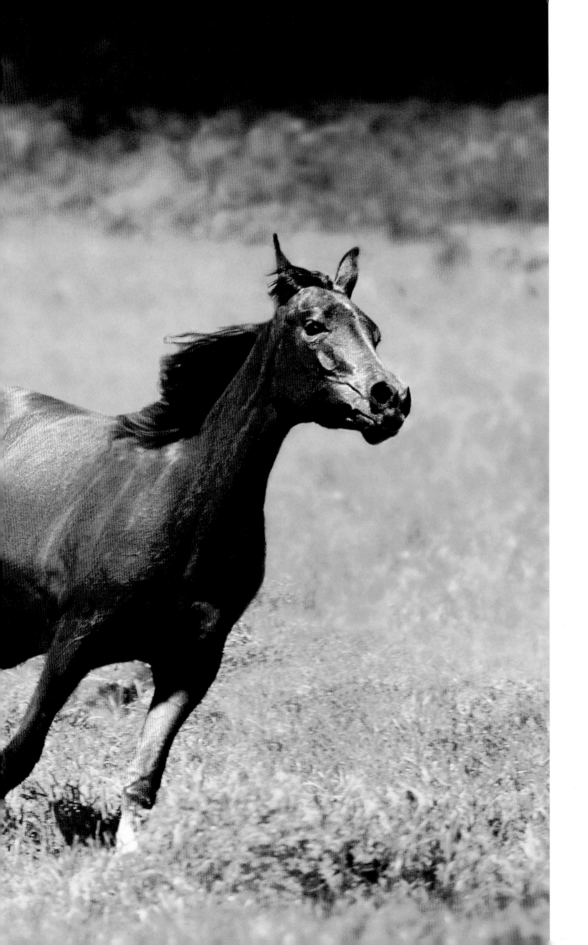

USA. Elegant and fast, Mustangs run free in the American prairies.

176-177 ● USA. A ford in South Dakota provides a chance to cool down and play.

178-179 ● USA. Headed by a herd leader, these wild horses cross a swollen river in South Dakota.

180-181 ● USA. Impetuous natures and harmony of movement: a group of Thoroughbreds against the big sky of Montana.

182-183 ● USA. Wyoming's long grass country encourages these colts and fillies in their instinctive tendency to run.

The STEEDS of the FUTURE

SENIO SENSI

● France. This Arabian foal's sweet face shows the grace and beauty of this breed.

INTRODUCTION The Steeds of the Future

I HAVE ALWAYS THOUGHT THAT ANIMALS HAVE A SECRET LIFE THAT NOT EVEN ETHOLOGY CAN EXPLAIN. THEY HAVE A LIFE OF EMOTIONS, SENTIMENTS, SORROWS AND JOY PERHAPS EQUAL TO OUR OWN. THE INNERMOST SECRET LIES IN THE BIRTH OF AN ANIMAL: WHEREAS A WOMAN CAN EXPLAIN, ASK AND IN-FORM, UNLESS THEY LEAVE NATURE TO LOOK AFTER ITSELF, ANI-MALS CAN ONLY LOOK AT US, ALMOST IMPLORINGLY, FOR SUP-PORT. QUITE BY CHANCE, I WAS ONCE PRESENT AT THE BIRTH OF A FARM HORSE; NEEDING A BREECH DELIVERY, THE FOAL RE-QUIRED ALL THE EXPERIENCE, ENERGY AND DELICACY OF THE VET AND FARMER SO THAT IT WOULD NOT DIE DURING THE BIRTH.

INTRODUCTION The Steeds of the Future

AS SOON AS THE PLACENTA DROPPED OUT OF THE MOTHER'S

BODY, SHE EXAMINED HER FOAL, AND SNIFFED AND LICKED IT.

THE TINY NEWCOMER ATTEMPTED TO STAND UP BUT CLUMSILY

FELL OVER. IT WAS MORE FORTUNATE A LITTLE LATER WHEN IT

SEARCHED FOR ITS MOTHER'S TEAT AND BEGAN TO SUCK. GAN-

GLING AND A LITTLE COMICAL, ITS LONG LEGS AND TINY BODY

MADE IT RESEMBLE A BOY THAT HAD GROWN TOO QUICKLY.

FOAL: THE OFFSPRING OF A HORSE. A TINY FOAL: THE DEFINITION

OF TENDERNESS. FOALS SHOULD ALWAYS HAVE A CHILD CLOSE

BY FOR RECIPROCAL BENEFIT: SO THAT THE CHILD WILL LEARN

TO RESPECT ANIMALS AND THE FOAL WILL HAVE A LESS TRAU-

The Steeds of the Future

Introduction

MATIC EXPERIENCE WHEN IT COMES TO BE TRAINED, AS, THOUGH THIS IS A STANDARD OCCURRENCE, IT IS AN UNNATURAL ONE. A FOAL IS THE SYMBOL OF JOYOUS FREEDOM. IT PLAYS IN ITS FIELD WITHOUT LOGIC OR RULES, THEN RETURNS TO ITS MOTHER TO LEARN AND IMITATE PROUDLY HER PHYSICAL MOVE-MENTS. WATCHING A FOAL AND ITS MOTHER I SOMETIMES WON-DER WHAT TYPE OF COMMUNICATION LINKS THE TWO OTHER THAN TEACHING BY EXAMPLE. TEACHING A YOUNGSTER HOW TO LIVE ITS LIFE IS DIFFICULT FOR ONE AND ALL, BUT MORE SO TO THOSE WHO ARE SUBJECTED TO THE DEMANDS OF MAN. PER-HAPS THIS IS A SECRET THAT IT IS BETTER NOT TO FIND OUT.

● France. An Arabian colt explores the world as he develops his independence.

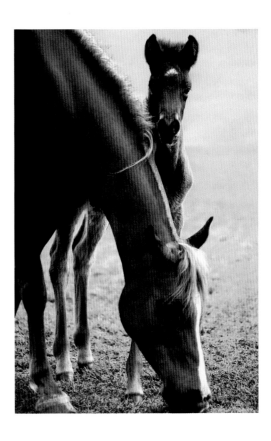

190-191 ● Austria. A palomino-coated Haflinger coat seems to draw a sense of security from his mother's proximity.

191 ● France. While his mother feeds, the small Arabian remains close by; he is almost fearful.

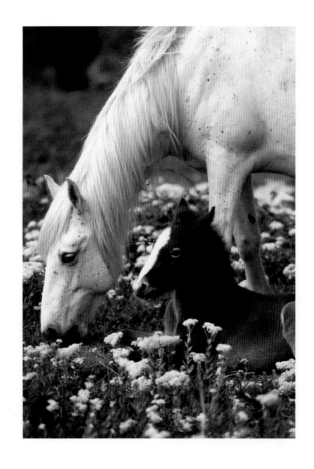

192 and 193 ● France. With its mother, the foal learns to distinguish edible herbs.

194-195 ● Great Britain. A tiny Shetland plays with his mother, helping to develop his muscles.

196 ● France. The mother-child bond is very strong among horses.

197 ● Asia. Mother and foal of the Przewalski breed in a pose of tender "complicity."

● USA. Two foals rest happily in a soft, grassy meadow. A foal's life includes wild, scatty gallops and deep sleeps.

200-201 ● Iceland. This little Iceland pony doesn't seem to want to wander far from his mother.

201 ● Great Britain. A young Shetland pony comfortably asleep in a field.

202-203 ● Austria. The foals of many species – in this case a Haflinger – gradually lose the down they have when they are born.

Great Britain. Two colts play freely: moments like these help to teach them jumping movements.

● Great Britain. A pair of foals
frolics close to the adults of the
herd; they gaze at each other,
discovering the world around
them together.

208 and 209 ● Germany. The first neighs of two very young foals: communication is fundamental in the animal world.

210-211 ● Iceland. This Iceland pony seems to be hiding behind his mother's reassuring bulk.

● USA. A foal trots and then rests in a colorful field.

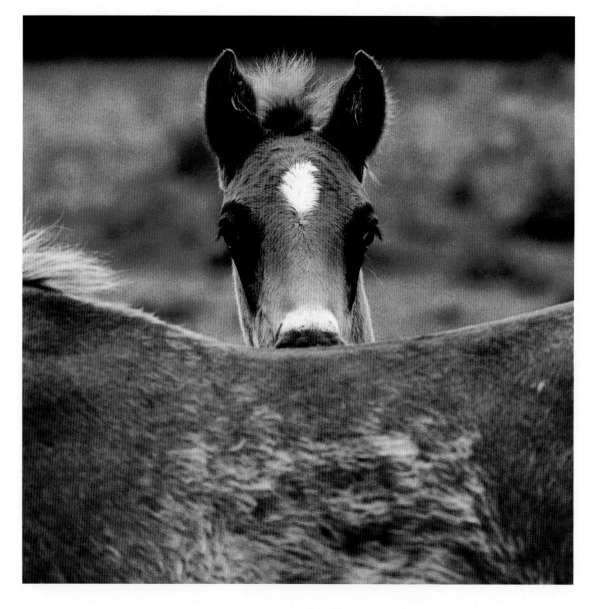

214 and 215 ● Great Britain. Foals need constant contact with the adults in the herd.

216-217 ● Germany. A Shetland pony adopts the most extreme – and comical – way to scratch its back.

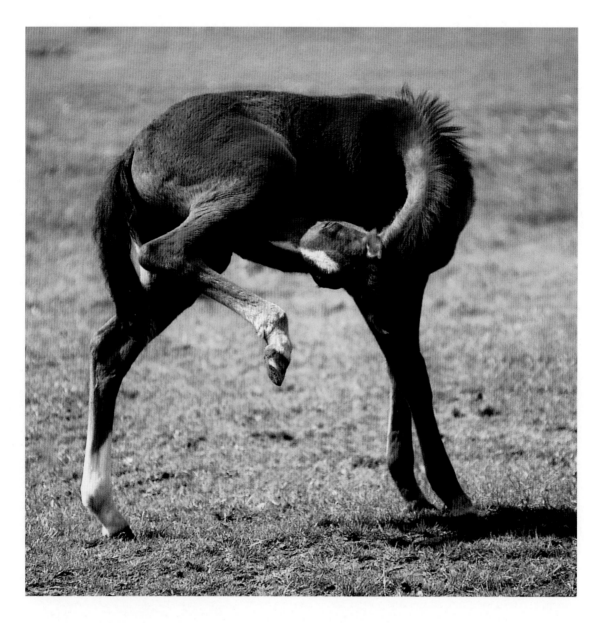

Germany. Two foals concentrate on cleaning themselves. Their sense of touch is so highly developed that even a fly landing anywhere on their body is enough to trigger a reaction.

220 ● USA. Long, slender legs, clearly out of proportion to their bodies, help foals move with a minimum of agility and speed.

221 ● France. An Appaloosa cares for and cleans his coat.

222 ● Great Britain. A baby Gypsy Vanner stretches his legs in playful jumps next to an adult.

223 ● Great Britain. A lovely dappled colt bucks energetically, its movements showing remarkable natural elegance.

Germany. A Friesian colt, already looking as haughty as an adult of the breed, stands near its mother.

Great Britain. On the left, an Arabian looks at a kitten; on the right, a Shetland pony curiously watches an egret.

228 ● Great Britain. A tranquil trot for these colts that are familiarizing themselves with the world around them.

229 ● Ireland. The mother of a tiny Irish pony teaches her youngster to run in the open space.

" THE CONDITION OF FOALS IS SINGULAR, AS THEY ARE THE GAWKY OFFSPRING OF WHAT WE PERCEIVE AS THE MOST GRACEFUL CREATURES ON EARTH. THIS MAKES THEM ALL THE MORE TOUCHING TO OBSERVE AS THEY DETERMINEDLY FOLLOW THEIR PARENTS' EXAMPLE TO FACE WHAT WE CAN EASILY DEFINE AS A METAMORPHOSIS RATHER THAN NORMAL GROWTH. "

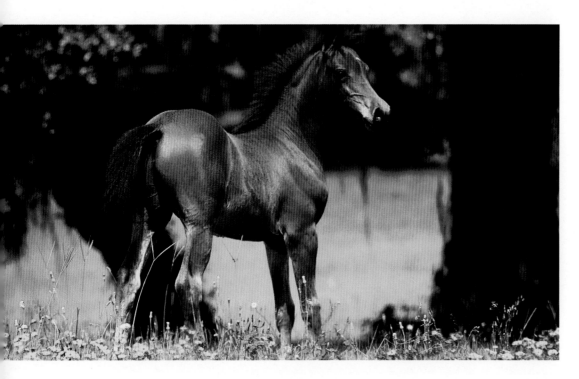

● Great Britain. Two colts enjoy their contact with nature in complete solitude.

232 ● Germany. There is a long tradition of breeding Arabian foals: the Bedouins considered them a priceless treasure.

233 ● Germany. Arabian foals show all the breed's sense of pride and elegance, but on a smaller scale.

● Germany. A mother lavishes care and attention on her foal. As a rule, horses are extremely affectionate and sensitive: "friendly" in the full sense of the word.

USA. A Criollo mother and foal nuzzle each other affectionately. These are very sturdy and reliable horses that are used to the open spaces of the pampas.

● USA. An Arabian foal suckles his mother. After the birth, a foal will normally be able to stand within an hour, and the first thing he does is to drink his mother's rich milk.

240-241 ● Great Britain. A gray-coated Arabian lavishes attention on her bay foal. The rarest color for foals of this breed is all black.

242-243 ● Great Britain. An entire family runs in the meadow: this is an excellent exercise for the growth of young foals and fillies.

244 ● Germany. Foals communicate on various levels. Even the position of their ears, erect and relaxed as here, is significant.

245 ● Germany. The sense of smell is the most important one in social relations among foals. As they smell, they often raise their upper lip slightly.

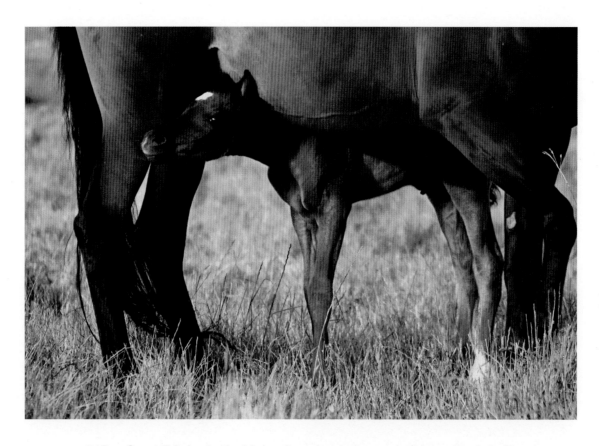

246 ● Great Britain. An Arabian colt seeks shelter under his mother's belly.

247 ● Germany. Ponies often turn to their mothers, as they seek their attention
for something or simply want to run and frolic.

• Iceland. A small Iceland pony tries every position imaginable to rest.
Here, though the pony seems to be grazing, it is actually dozing.

MUZZLES and WHINNIES

GABRIELE BOISELLE

251 ● Iceland. The Palomino pony almost looks angry. In reality, this kind of grimace is referred to as the Flehman reflex, and it is connected with olfactory perception.

253 ● Austria. Haflingers are generally very gentle by nature but during the mating season aggressiveness and fighting is seen more frequently.

INTRODUCTION Muzzles and Whinnies

MY PROFESSION AS A PHOTOGRAPHER BRINGS ME CLOS-

ER TO MORE DIFFERENT TYPES OF HORSE THAN ALMOST ANYBODY

ELSE CAN HOPE TO MEET. THERE ARE THE TIMID ONES AND THE RUDE

ONES, THE ARROGANT ONES AND THE "MACHOS." I CAN NEVER TELL

WHICH CHARACTER WILL POP UP IN FRONT OF MY LENS. AND I AM AL-

WAYS ANXIOUSLY LOOKING FORWARD TO DISCOVER GREAT NEW PER-

SONALITIES ON MY PHOTO-SHOOTS – AND MOST OFTEN SUCCEED.

SOMETIMES I REALLY HAVE TO WATCH OUT. ONCE I PHOTOGRAPHED

ANSATA NILE PASCHA, A WELL-REGARDED CHAMPION ARABIAN STAL-

LION. THIS VERY SPECIAL HORSE HAD SEEN IT ALL, ALL THE SHOW

RINGS OF THE WORLD, BOTH SIDES OF THE OCEAN IN AMERICA AND

INTRODUCTION Muzzles and Whinnies

EUROPE. HE WAS JUST FED UP WITH ALL THE CRUELLY BURDENSOME

DEMANDS OF THE TRAINERS AND WAS BEGGING TO BE A NORMAL

HORSE OUT IN THE FIELD. BUT BEING TO VALUABLE HE HAD TO GO TO

WORK AND HATED IT. AND HE HATED ALL THE PEOPLE WEARING

DRESSED UP IN WHITE FOR A PERFORMANCE OR STRUTTING AROUND

CARRYING A WHIP IN THEIR HANDS. UNFORTUNATELY, THAT DAY I WAS

IN WHITE WITH MY CAMERA IN MY HAND – AND THAT DID NOT LOOK

GOOD TO THE STALLION. SO HE CAME TOWARD, EYES BLAZING,

TEETH BARED. FOR A MOMENT, MY BREATHING FROZE; I KNEW I

WOULD NOT BE FAST ENOUGH TO ESCAPE THROUGH THE FENCE.

TRUSTING TO THE INSTINCTS I HAD DEVELOPED WITH HORSES, I DID

INTRODUCTION Muzzles and Whinnies

NOT WAIT UNTIL HE HAD REACHED ME, BUT SPRANG FORWARD TO-

WARD HIM LIKE AN ATTACKING FORCE. HE WAS SO TAKEN BY SUR-

PRISE THAT HE JUMPED ASIDE, STOPPED AND TURNED AROUND WITH

AN EXPRESSIONLESS FACE, ASKING "WHAT WAS THAT??? THEN HE

CAREFULLY STEPPED CLOSER, AS IF ASKING "HALLO! WHO ARE YOU?"

SO, I HAD BROKEN HIS BARRIER OF HATE. I PUT MY CAMERA ASIDE

AND WE PLAYED AROUND FOR ABOUT HALF AN HOUR IN THE PAS-

TURE – HE HAD FUN WITH ME. HE WAS ONE OF THE MOST PERFECT

MODELS I HAVE EVER HAD AND AS GENTLE AND COOPERATING AS

YOU COULD IMAGINE . . . SO LONG AS NONE OF HIS TRAINERS

SHOWED UP. I'VE LEARNED ONE LESSON IN MY JOB: NEVER TRUST

Muzzles and Whinnies
Introduction

THE WORD OF PEOPLE ABOUT HORSES. YOU MUST YOURSELF DIS-

COVER THE MAKE-UP OF THE HORSE IN FRONT OF YOU: INSIDE AND

OUTSIDE. AND I NEVER FOUND A REALLY MEAN HORSE THAT WAS NOT

MADE MEAN BY MAN. HORSES ARE THE MOST NOBLE AND SPIRITUAL

CREATURES I HAVE EVER MET IN MY LIFE. I HAVE SEEN HORSES BEAT-

EN UP AND MISTREATED YET STILL FAITHFUL AND LOYAL. I HAVE SEEN

HORSES CARING FOR THEIR HANDICAPPED RIDERS, LIKE FOR THEIR

OWN CHILDREN. I AM BLESSED TO BE ABLE TO DISCOVER THE WORLD

OF HORSES AGAIN AND AGAIN, TO LEARN SO MUCH ABOUT THEM –

AND TO ADORE THEM MORE AND MORE.

● Iceland. Iceland ponies being demonstrative. Horses are social animals
and hate to be alone.

● Argentina. Criollo stallions fiercely defending their mares. The winner will lead the entire herd.

Argentina. Determined and independent, Criollo stallions have a very strong character amply demonstrated in their "fiery" behavior.

● Argentina. A Criollo stallion demonstrates his physical strength.

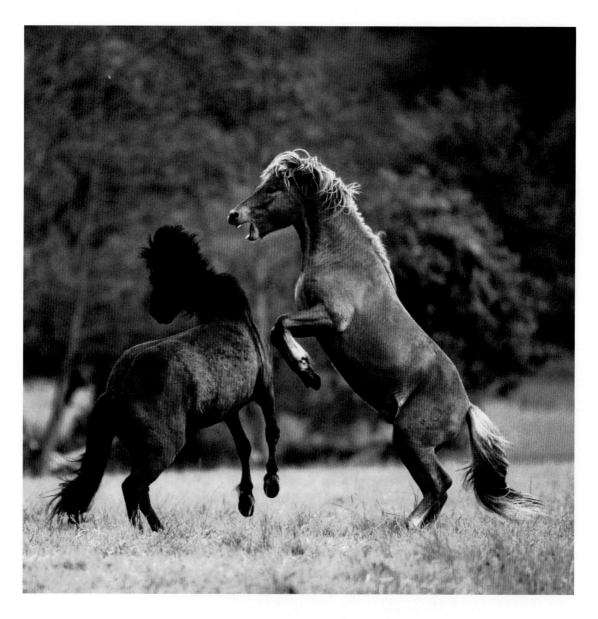

Germany. A bay and sorrel use their physical strength trying
to defeat one another.

● Austria. Two Haflingers battle to win the leadership of the herd. In this struggle, each horse tries to defeat the other, using its robust jaws and kicking with its front legs in the attempt.

268 ● France. The bay clearly seems to have got the better of his adversary.

269 ● The Netherlands. Fighting between horses, Friesians in this case, may not be "to the death," but can nevertheless be violent.

270 ● Austria. A dramatic fight between two Haflinger ponies.

271 ● The Netherlands. A Friesian expresses the sheer joy of freedom with spontaneous enthusiasm.

272 ● Ireland. Gypsy Vanners are athletically built, which makes them well suited to riding and dressage.

272-273 ● Great Britain. Bred horses, in this case a Gypsy Vanner, need just as much freedom and open space as their wild cousins.

● Iceland. Two Iceland ponies show their teeth in an act of defiance. If tamed early, this breed is very gentle.

● France.
France. A horse from
the Camargue seems
to have relished its
meal. Wild horses eat
only a little at a time,
but often.

278-279 ● Egypt. An Arabian energetically scratches its back in the dust.

279 ● The Netherlands. A black Friesian finds relief from the insects by rolling on the ground.

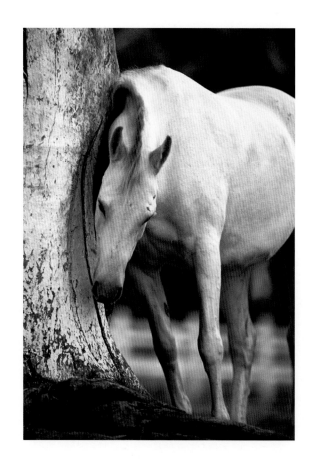

Spain. Andalusian horses rub against a tree trunk. Regardless of where they live, horses must deal with an ever-present torment: insects.

● France.
France. A stockade
becomes a welcome
source of relief for this
wild horse tormented by
itchiness.

● Italy. These horses behave tenderly toward each other during the courting season.

● Spain.
Two Spanish horses
show affectionate
behavior. This breed, with
a noble appearance and
character, is very strong
and athletic and can be
tamed with great ease.

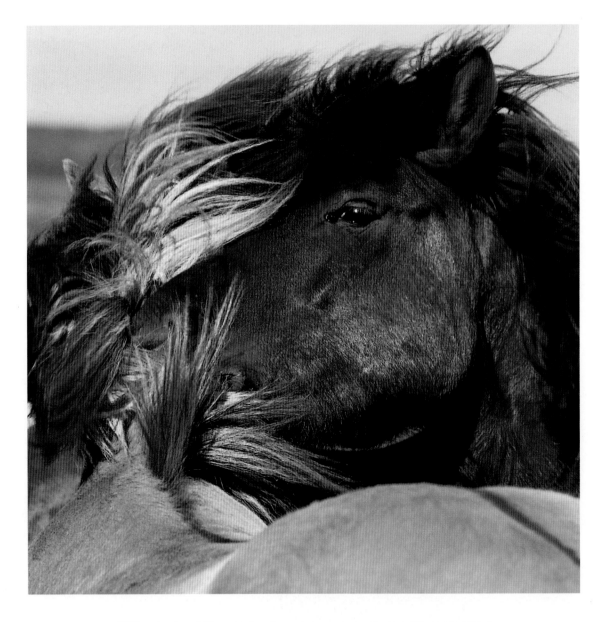

288 ● Iceland. Two Iceland ponies seek contact with each other.

289 ● Hungary. Shagya Arabians are tender towards one another.

Austria. Horses detest
solitude, so they are often
seen side by side in pairs,
like these two Haflingers.

LIFE on the RANCH

MEDFORD TAYLOR

USA. A cowboy and his horse show off in a wild vault.

INTRODUCTION Life on the Ranch

"YEE HA! . . . HERE THEY COME." DISTANT HOOFBEATS BREAK THE DAWN ON ASSATEAGUE ISLAND, VIRGINIA. SUDDENLY, FROM OUT OF THE FOG HANGING LOW OVER THE SALT MARSHES AND DUNES, HORSES APPEAR, POUNDING THEIR WAY ACROSS THE SAND. ON THIS JULY MORNING, "SALTWATER" COWBOYS MOVE THE NORTH-ERN HERD OF WILD HORSES TOWARD THE OCEAN FOR A TWO-MILE TROT ALONG THE BEACH AND THEN THE CHANNEL SWIM TO CHIN-COTEAGUE. THIS IS THE START OF THE ANNUAL PONY PENNING. DUR-ING ONE WEEK EVERY YEAR, A GROUP OF MEN FROM A VARIETY OF PROFESSIONS MEET UP FOR THE WILD HORSE ROUNDUP. AND FOR

● Italy. A Tuscan hand tends the herd.

INTRODUCTION Life on the Ranch

THIS BRIEF TIME IN SUMMER THEY BECOME SALTWATER COWBOYS, AND PARTICIPATE IN A TRADITIONAL ROUNDUP THAT HAS LASTED FOR NEARLY 80 YEARS. 'I GREW UP DREAMING OF BEING A COWBOY AND LOVING THE COWBOY WAYS . . . PURSUING THE LIFE OF MY HIGH-RID-ING HEROES.' THESE WORDS, FROM THE WILLIE NELSON SONG "MY HEROES HAVE ALWAYS BEEN COWBOYS," COULD BE THE DREAM OF EVERY BOY WHO GREW UP GOING TO COWBOY MOVIES AS I DID. WEARING MY TOY SIX-GUNS, I WOULD RELIVE THE MOVIE ON MY WALK BACK HOME FROM THE THEATER, IN THE SOUTHERN TOWN WHERE I GREW UP. MANY YEARS LATER AS A PHOTOGRAPHER ON ASSIGN-MENT, I LAY ON MY SWAG UNDER THE STARS OF THE AUSTRALIAN OUT-BACK . . . ON A REAL CATTLE MUSTER, WITH REAL COWBOYS . . .

INTRODUCTION Life on the Ranch

RINGERS, DOWN UNDER, MATE. I WAS AT PEACE . . . A BOYHOOD

DREAM COME TRUE.

THE CREATION OF THE MYTHIC COWBOY PERSONA BY POPULAR CUL-

TURE IS NOT CONFINED TO THE AMERICAN COWBOY – THE COWBOY

IS A UNIVERSALLY ADMIRED LEGEND. IN MEXICO, HE'S CALLED VAQUE-

RO. THE *GAUCHOS* OF ARGENTINA, URUGUAY AND BRAZIL STILL RIDE

PROUDLY; ONCE CALLED THE 'WANDERERS OF THE PAMPAS,' *GAU-*

CHOS ARE A RESPECTED SYMBOL OF THEIR COUNTRIES HERITAGE. IN

AUSTRALIA THE COWBOYS ARE RINGERS, JACKAROOS AND JILLA-

ROOS, AND THEY LIVE AN INDEPENDENT AND RUGGED EXISTENCE. THE

BUTTERO IS ITALY'S COWBOY. ALONG CENTRAL ITALY'S WESTERN

BORDERS, IN TUSCANY, LIES THE HIDDEN FRONTIER OF MAREMMA. AN

INTRODUCTION Life on the Ranch

ALMOST MYTHICAL PLACE OF OPEN PLAINS AND FORESTS, MAREMMA

IS HOME TO THE LAST OF THE BUTTERI. THERE ARE FEW WILD HORSES

OR CATTLE LEFT, BUT MANY OF THE BUTTERI'S TRADITIONS ARE KEPT

ALIVE THROUGH EVENTS SPONSORED BY BUTTERI D'ALTA MAREMMA,

INCLUDING THE ANNUAL TRANSHUMANCE, A TWO-DAY WILD-HORSE

ROUNDUP ACROSS THE TUSCAN LANDSCAPE. A COWBOY AND HIS

HORSE ARE AS ONE. TOGETHER THEY DO A JOB. THEY WORK AS A

TEAM THROUGH DRIVING RAIN, DUST STORMS, BLIZZARDS OR BAKING

SUN. A COWBOY LOVES HIS HORSE BECAUSE HE IS LOYAL AND CAR-

RIES HIM THROUGH THE BEST AND THE WORST OF TIMES, AND HE IS

ALWAYS DILIGENT, NO MATTER HOW TIRED FROM HOURS UNDER THE

SADDLE. A CENTURY AGO, A COWBOY AND HIS HORSE COULD RIDE

INTRODUCTION Life on the Ranch

THOUSANDS OF MILES ON ONE CATTLE DRIVE. TODAY THE AMERICAN WEST HAS BOUNDARIES, FENCES AND INTERSTATE HIGHWAYS. CATTLE ARE MOVED IN TERMS OF DAYS, NOT WEEKS OR MONTHS. IN AUSTRALIA, RINGERS NOW TAKE A FEW DAYS TO DRIVE CATTLE TO THE ROAD TRAINS, WHERE BEFORE IT WOULD TAKE WEEKS TO REACH A RAILHEAD. THE COWBOY'S WAY OF LIFE HAS CHANGED JUST LIKE EVERYONE ELSE'S. BUT FOR THE REST OF US, IT IS THE COWBOY'S WAY OF LIFE THAT WE ADMIRE. IT IS THEIR LIFE THAT WE ROMANTICIZE ABOUT, BECAUSE A COWBOY REPRESENTS INDEPENDENCE, ADVENTURE AND WIDE OPEN SPACES. A VAQUERO, *GAUCHO*, BUTTERO, JACKAROO, OR BUCKAROO — THEY ARE PART OF EACH COUNTRY'S HERITAGE, AND WE LOVE THEM FOR THEIR TENACITY TO SURVIVE IN

Life on the Ranch
Introduction

CHANGING TIMES. BACK ON CHINCOTEAGUE, THE COLTS AND YEAR-

LINGS HAVE BEEN SOLD AT AUCTION, AND THE SALTWATER COWBOYS

DRIVE THE HORSES DOWN NARROW STREETS OF THIS ISLAND TOWN.

THEY'RE HEADING BACK TO THE WATER TO SWIM THE CHANNEL

HOME TO ASSATEAGUE ISLAND. WET COATS GLISTEN IN THE SUN AS

THEY RISE FROM THE WATER AND THEIR HOOVES HIT FAMILIAR SAND

AND MUD. WATCHING THE HORSES SHAKE THEIR MANES AND RUN

FREE AGAIN YOU CAN ONLY HAVE A FEELING OF GRATITUDE, KNOWING

THE HERD WILL STILL BE THERE NEXT YEAR WHEN THE SALTWATER

COWBOYS RETURN.

● Argentina. Getting a herd across a river is a tough job: horses are delicate animals.

USA. Shoeing a horse requires skill and precision.

304-305 ● USA. The lasso is an everyday work tool for a cowboy.

305 ● USA. Keeping a herd of wild horses under control requires constant movement.

306-307 ● USA. Horses are led into the enclosure.

307 ● USA. The animals on a ranch are kept clean and healthy.

308 and 308-309 ● USA. Enclosure gates are made from simple poles that can be lifted out of the ground.

310-311 ● USA. Two cowboys break into a gallop in front of the mountains of Utah.

USA. A hand leads the herd as he loops his lasso in the air.

USA. A racing group of
wild horses is a
breathtaking sight.

316 ● USA. Boots and spurs are typical wear for cowboys.

316-317 ● USA. Other important pieces of clothing are suede leg protectors called chaps.

Canada. A blacksmith forges horseshoes in the semidarkness of his workshop. Life on the ranch follows age-old rhythms.

● USA. Horses are of major
importance in controlling herds
of cattle.

● USA. Working with horses not only requires strength but also qualities such as sensitivity and awareness.

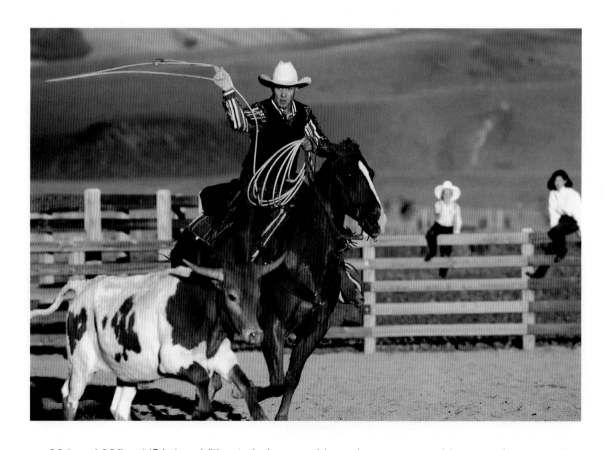

324 and 325 ● USA. In addition to being capable and courageous riders, cowboys must also be very agile and have great manual ability in order to handle the lasso correctly.

326-327 ● USA. A group of horses gallops freely outside the pen.

328-329 ● USA. The herd is checked every day, rain or shine.

from 330 to 335 ● USA. Canyons, cowboys and wild horses are iconic images of the American West and its untrammeled freedoms.

336-337 ● USA. Working in pairs makes following the animals easier.

338-339 ● USA. Watched over by a herder, the livestock move on in an orderly manner.

340-341 ● USA. Wide
open spaces and the
open sky are appealing
traits of the cowboy's
work

from 342 to 345 ● USA.
A vigilant eye needs to
be kept when the herd is
grazing or in the ring.

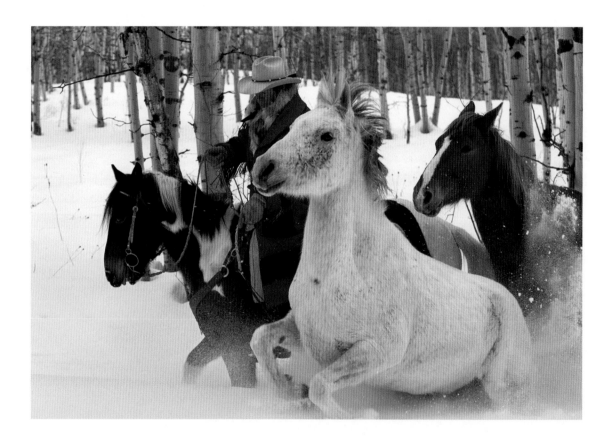

346 and 347 ● USA. Cowboys and horses have a hard time picking their way through the fresh snow. The Pinto, Quarterhorse and Appaloosa are the breeds preferred by cowboys because of their stamina and docile temperament.

348-349 ● USA. Cowboys have to handle the harshness of nature and the elements.

350-351 ● Argentina. Led by the *gaucho*, who is barely visible in the upper part of the picture, a herd of Criollos briskly fords a torrent on the pampa.

from 352 to 355 ●
Argentina. *Gauchos*
watch the herd from
behind for a better view.

● Mexico. Lasso in hand to intimidate the cattle, the herdsmen rides along at the edge of the herd, close enough to keep it from dispersing.

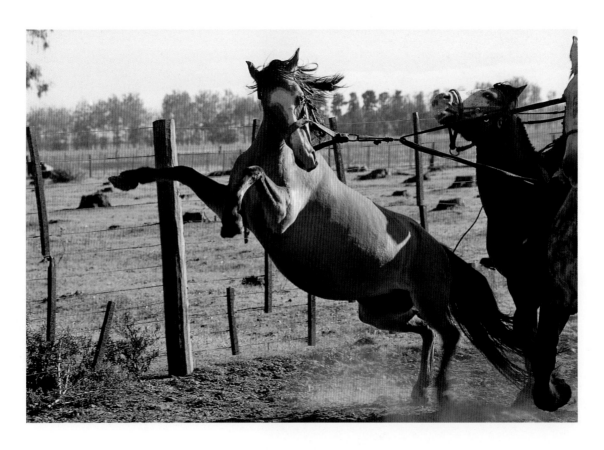

358 ● Argentina. Criollos are difficult to train, and the presence of an already
trained one often helps the process.

359 ● Argentina. Two *domadores* at work in the pen.

360-361 ● Argentina. The *domador*, who faces serious risks in his work,
is a highly respected figure.

362-363 ● Argentina. Two *gauchos* recover a calf in difficulty.

363 and 364-365 ● Argentina. Fording rivers is a dramatic moment, often dangerous for men and horses.

366-367 ● Argentina. Two *gauchos* steer a herd of Criollos by whirling short crops called *rebenques*.

368 and 369 ● Italy. Tuscany's superb countryside is a fitting backdrop to these working herders.

370-371 ● Italy. Like other herdsmen around the world, the *butteri* work with horses every day, developing a very special rapport of equality and friendship.

" **F**OR HERDSMEN AROUND THE WORLD AND THOSE WHO LIVE WITH LIVESTOCK EVERY DAY, THE HORSE MEANS WORK, FATIGUE AND SWEAT – RAIN OR SHINE – AND SLEEPING OUT IN THE OPEN. AT THE SAME TIME, HOWEVER, IT ALSO IMPLIES THE KIND OF FREEDOM DREAMED BY MANY AND ENJOYED BY FEW. "

from 372 to 375 ● Italy. In the Maremma, the *butteri's* horse is accustomed to living semi-wild in the country, alongside the longhorn cattle typical of the region.

Italy. The first step in training the Maremmana is handled without a saddle, working inside the pen.

378-379 ● France. The *gardians*, the herdsmen of the Camargue, follow a young bull. The cattle are raised in freedom in order to run during the traditional festivals of Provence.

380-381 ● France. A group of *gardians* precedes a large herd of cattle of the Camargue. The man in the middle grips the tool of this trade, the long handle of the *trident*.

Spain. A *doma vaqueras* follows the herd, which moves at rapid speed.

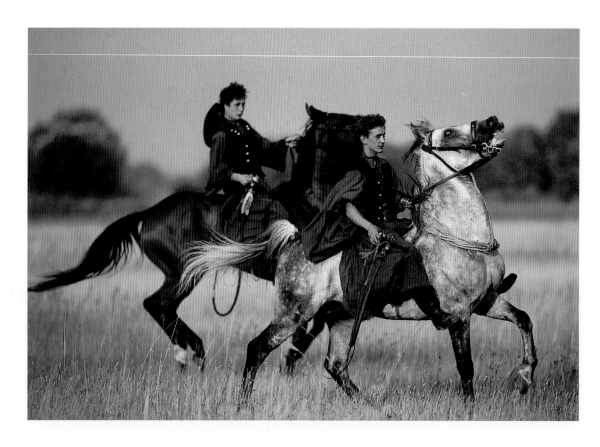

● Hungary. The thrilling spectacle of the *czikos*, the highly skilled Hungarian herdsmen, enlivens the *puszta*'s monotonous landscape.

● Hungary. A *czikos*, dressed in the traditional oversized blue shirt, guides a herd of magnificent bays across the *puszta*.

from 388 to 391 ●
Mongolia. Mongolian stockhands have to brave very low temperatures in wide open spaces.

● Australia. The
Australian working
cowboy's environment is
usually huge, dry, dusty
expanses.

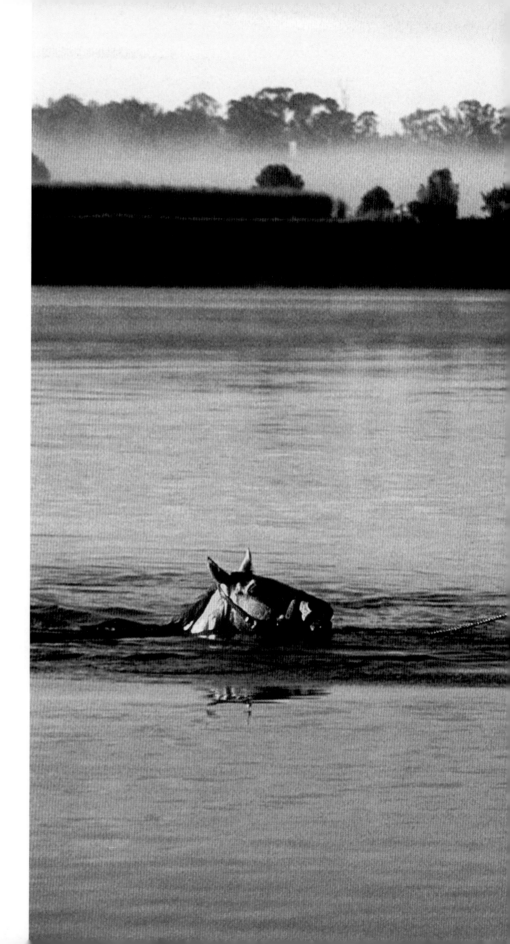

394-395 ● Australia.
A boat and cable are vital
tools is bringing this
horse across a broad
river.

396-397 ● Australia.
The cowboys' gait slows
up to match that of their
herds. It reflects the
traditional – or "natural " –
tempo of their calling.

Australia. Sun and dust accompany the herdsmen's daily work. In Australia, cowboys are referred to by various names, such as *jackaroos*, *jillaroos*, or *ringers*.

CHILDREN and HORSES

PAOLO MANILI

● India. A very young Buddhist novice looks after a Mongolian horse.

INTRODUCTION Children and Horses

Not all children like horses. Some are frightened of their size or, more simply, they prefer other animals like dogs, cats and rabbits, etc. On the other hand, there are children who like horses before they have even seen one. This attraction may result from their education, children's stories, cartoons or simply their own character. Such children are extraordinarily interested in horses and, when they first encounter one, an alchemy occurs that not even experts are able to define. This fascination is returned by horses that recognize that the young humans before them are not predators to flee but simply the

INTRODUCTION Children and Horses

'FOALS' OF ANOTHER SPECIES. IN ONE OF THE MYSTERIOUS LAWS OF

NATURE, OFTEN EVEN SKITTISH HORSES ARE ATTENTIVE AND SHOW

DELICACY TOWARD CHILDREN. THIS EXTRAORDINARY ANIMAL EXERTS

A STRONG APPEAL ON PEOPLE, IN PARTICULAR THOSE WITH GREAT

IMAGINATION: THE 'NOBLE QUADRUPED' CELEBRATED BY ARTISTS

REPRESENTS BEAUTY AND GRACE, STRENGTH AND HUMAN DREAMS.

THEY STIMULATE THE IMAGINATION, DESIRE AND THE DESIRE FOR POS-

SESSION. CHILDREN LOVE BEAUTY, THEY DREAM WITH OPEN EYES,

WANTING THINGS THAT THEY LIKE. THEN, ONCE THEIR INTEREST IS RE-

CIPROCATED, A LOVE SWELLS INSIDE THEM FOR THIS LARGE, APPRE-

CIATIVE CREATURE, SO FRIENDLY THAT IT MIGHT BE A GIANT TOY. THIS

Children and Horses
Introduction

SIMILARITY TO A TOY HAS BEEN TAKEN AS THE BASIS FOR THE MOST

RECENT METHOD OF TEACHING VERY YOUNG CHILDREN TO RIDE. IN

COUNTRIES WHERE EQUESTRIANISM IS ADVANCED, CHILDREN START

TO LEARN RIDING ON PONIES RATHER THAN HORSES FOR A MORE

BALANCED RELATIONSHIP BETWEEN SIZE AND STRENGTH, AND THEY

APPROACH COMPETITIVE RIDING THROUGH PONY GAMES. IN THE

WEST PONY-RIDING COMPETITIONS ARE VERY COMMON AND EVEN

HAVE AN INTERNATIONAL CALENDAR; THE BEST RIDERS ARE ELIGIBLE

TO ENTER EUROPEAN AND WORLD CHAMPIONSHIPS IN VARIOUS DISCI-

PLINES AND ARE LIKELY TO GO ON TO BECOME FUTURE CHAMPIONS.

405 ● USA. A young rider carefully guides her pet to the ranch.

406-407 ● USA. A budding cowboy simulates a rodeo performance under
the eyes of a 'real' cowboy.

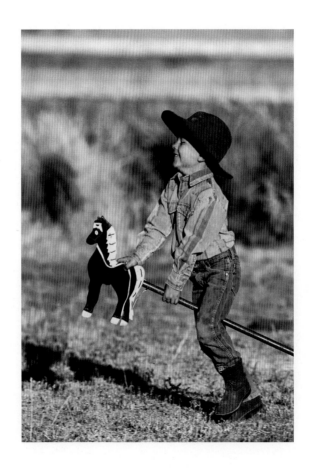

408 • USA. Whether made of wood or of real flesh and blood, a horse is a perfect play companion.

409 • USA. Tackling the rudiments of lassoing.

410-411 • USA. Before a rodeo, a young boy watches a horse with evident admiration.

USA. Youngsters together:
a boy and a colt gain confidence
as they study each other with
interest.

● Germany. A young rider shows her confidence in her magnificent Arabian. More than with other domesticated animals, human beings tend to treat horses as equals.

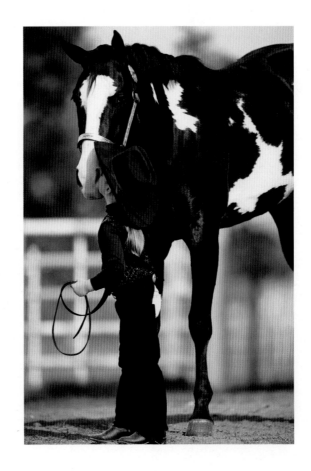

416 ● USA. An aspiring cowgirl in a matching outfit tenderly kisses her proud steed.

417 ● Ireland. A girl and a pony get to know one another. Horses love to be petted.

USA. Once initial wariness is dissolved (mostly caused by the difference in size), children place complete trust in horses – a trust that will not be betrayed.

Great Britain. The woolly shin-bones of a Shire are as tall as the squatting girl but she is not in any danger. Even the most skittish horses treat children with care.

422 ● Great Britain. Two young jockeys jump a hedge during a competition.

423 ● Great Britain. Falls are educational: a jockey slips from his saddle as he comes out of a jump.

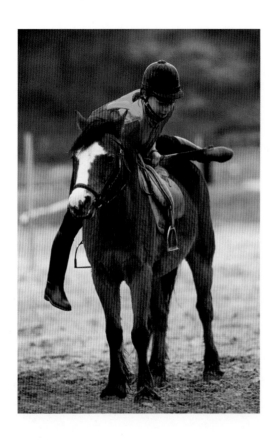

424 ● Italy. An aspiring jockey dismounts, with some difficulty, from the saddle.

424-425 ● Great Britain. The enthusiasm of young riders – and their ponies – is unleashed at the gallop during a gymkhana.

426 ● Great Britain. Wearing a cap and with her plaits in ribbons, a young girl waits for the start of a competition.

426-427 ● Great Britain. Jumping with style: learning is best done early.

428 and 429 ● Mongolia. Numbered participants at a horse-race in Mongolia prepare to start. The riders chosen are between 5 and 13 years of age because this ensures the ability of the horses is tested, not that of the riders.

430-431 ● Mongolia. Children and adults in the saddle of impressive young Mongolian horses accelerate into a gallop on the steppes.

HORSES in UNIFORM

HENRY DALLAL

- Great Britain. On the Queen's Birthday, celebrated in June, the troops of the Household Cavalry (the Queen's personal guard) draw near to Windsor Castle.

INTRODUCTION Horses in Uniform

New to London, I was awakened by the echoing sounds of some thirty horses trotting in the cobblestone streets of this city. Running over to the window, the sight and the sounds of the "four-legged soldiers" with their mounted troopers on "watering orders" in the early morning darkness sparked fascination in me. Thus began my journey to photograph the Household Cavalry Mounted Regiment, the British sovereign's ceremonial bodyguard, the elite of the world's mounted cavalry. Some 23,000 images later, with my book *PAGEANTRY AND PERFORMANCE* completed, I remained just as fascinated as when I first started this journey seven years ago. Britain is world-renowned in keep-

INTRODUCTION Horses in Uniform

ING ALIVE THE TRADITION OF THE WARHORSE OF YESTERYEAR IN ITS

BRILLIANT POMP AND CEREMONY. WE HAVE THE HOUSEHOLD CAVAL-

RY, THE KING'S TROOP ROYAL HORSE ARTILLERY, THE HONOURABLE

ARTILLERY COMPANY, AND NUMEROUS OTHER UNITS, AS WELL AS THE

ROYAL MEWS (STABLES) WITH ITS MUSEUM. SOME OTHER COUNTRIES

ALSO MAINTAIN THE TRADITION OF THE "UNIFORMED HORSE," WEAV-

ING IT IN THEIR CULTURE AND HISTORY. THERE IS THE GARDE REPUBLI-

CAIN IN FRANCE, THE PRESIDENT'S BODY GUARD IN PAKISTAN, AND IN

INDIA THE 61ST CAVALRY, AND IN CANADA THE ROYAL CANADIAN

MOUNTED POLICE. THE CLOSER I LOOKED AT THE HORSE, THE MORE

THERE WAS TO SEE AND MARVEL AT. BESIDES ITS SOFT VELVETY MUZ-

ZLE, EVERY HORSE HAS ITS INDIVIDUAL CHARACTER, PERSONALITY

INTRODUCTION Horses in Uniform

AND TEMPERAMENT. ON THE DAY OF AN EVENT SUCH AS THE QUEEN'S

BIRTHDAY PARADE, AN 'ARMADA' OF OVER 400 HORSES COME TO DU-

TY AND TOGETHER WITH THEIR MOUNTED RIDERS (WHO AS MODERN

SOLDIERS MAY HAVE JUST RETURNED FROM A BATTLE ZONE OR

PEACE-KEEPING DUTY) RADIATE THAT GALLANTRY AND A SENSE OF

PRIDE AND HONOR. EACH HORSE HAS BEEN TRAINED FOR MONTHS,

AND ON THAT DAY, GROOMED FOR HOURS. THEIR HOOFS HAVE BEEN

POLISHED; THE SOLES OF THEIR FEET POWDERED WITH WHITE CHALK.

TROOPER AND HORSE ARE BRIGHTLY UNIFORMED WITH HEAVY SAD-

DLES AND ACCOUTERMENTS, JUST AS IN DAYS OF CAVALRY BATTLES.

THE CRISP EARLY MORNING LIGHT, THE MIST, THE HORSES' WARM

BREATH VISIBLE IN THE AIR, ARE ALL PART OF THE EXPECTANCY. THE

INTRODUCTION Horses in Uniform

JINGLING AND CLANGING, AND THE OCCASIONAL COUGH OR NEIGH

AS THIS ARMY STANDS PATIENTLY IN RANK AND FILE WHILE THE COM-

MANDER INSPECTS EVERY HORSE AND MOUNTED SOLDIER, BONDED

AS ONE PROUD BEING WAITING TO GO ON PARADE TO ESCORT THE

SOVEREIGN, PROUD TO STEP FORWARD AND MARCH IN FRONT OF THE

WORLD. WHETHER PULLING THE HEAVY GUNS OR THE ROYAL COACH

THEY KNOW THE ROUTE, THE MOMENT, AND THE SOLEMNITY OF THE

OCCASION. THERE IS A TIME TO PLAY AND BUCK, AND THERE IS THE

REQUIREMENT TO STAND AT ATTENTION FOR HOURS. A COMPLETE

MOUNTED ORCHESTRA MARCHES PAST IN PERFECT STEP, THE MUSI-

CIANS OBEYING THE CONDUCTOR'S BATON AS HE RIDES ON THE LEAD

HORSE. THE HEAVY KETTLE DRUMS REVERBERATING WITH THE MU-

Horses in Uniform
Introduction

SIC'S BEAT, PLAYED BY A REINS-FREE DRUMMER, CAN BE IN A DIFFER-

ENT TEMPO TO THE PACE OF THE MARCH. THROUGH THE LOUDLY

CHEERING AND CLAPPING CROWD, BELOW THE HELICOPTERS CIR-

CLING OVERHEAD, THE ARMADA OF NEARLY 400 HORSES PROUDLY

PERFORM, MAINTAINING THE STRICTEST DISCIPLINE. JUST OCCASION-

ALLY A PARTICULAR HORSE DECIDES, REGARDLESS OF HIS RIDERS

RANK OR TITLE, HAS IT NO BUSINESS BEING IN THE ROYAL PROCES-

SION, AND THUS BEGINS HIS OWN SOLO PARADE, USUALLY AT A

SWIFTER PACE AND IN A DIFFERENT DIRECTION, BUT EVENTUALLY TO

THE PLACE WHERE HE IS FED. . . .

• Italy. The horseback band of the Carabinieri parade down Via dei Fori Imperiali in Rome.

Great Britain

440-441 ● Great Britain. The Life Guards here are seen walking in a circle at the end of the parade.

441 ● Great Britain. Roll-call for the Life Guards: the horses and their riders are subjected to an exhausting discipline.

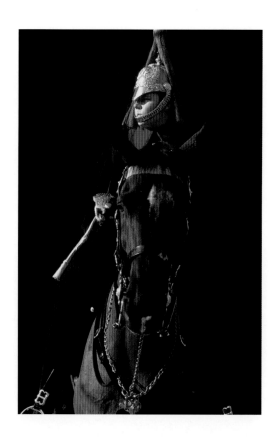

442 ● Great Britain. A Horse Guard awaits orders.

442-443 ● Great Britain. Saddles and harness as splendid as on the days of battle: everything must be perfect to honor the royal household.

Great Britain. Tiny details, like the shine on the boots and stirrups, receive a maximum amount of attention. Note the regimental monogram inscribed on the hoof.

● Great Britain. Wearing tunics embroidered with the Queen's monogram, musicians of the magnificent military band that accompanies the Trooping the Colour are able to play rhythms completely different to that of the march.

448-449 ● Great Britain. The Blues and Royals follow the Life Guards out of Windsor Castle.

449 ● Great Britain. Regiments assemble in Windsor Castle's vast Quadrangle.

Italy

Italy. With the eternal
Colosseum as a
backdrop, the Carabinieri
of the Cuirassier unit
parade in Via dei Fori
Imperiali during the Festa
della Repubblica.

452 ● Italy. Drawn up in Piazza di Siena in Rome, the mounted Carabinieri await the start of the exciting Carosello.

453 ● Italy. Quadrilles of horseback Carabinieri perform changing formations during the Carosello, reproducing movements of troops in battle.

454-455 ● Italy. The Fanfara of the Carabinieri files past during the Festa della Repubblica in Rome.

Italy. A company of mounted Carabinieri break into a gallop in the park at Villa Borghese in Rome.

France

France. On July 14th, the festival that marks the fall of the Bastille, a sea of shiny helmets fills the Avenue des Champs Elysées. This is the Garde Republicaine on parade.

460 ● France. The gleaming helmet of this Garde Républicaine cavalryman reflects the French sky.

461 ● The Garde Républicaine's fanfare parades in front of the Louvre.

Spain

462 ● Spain. A Spanish Civil Guard on service in the streets of Madrid.

462-463 ● Spain. Horseback guards present their lances in Plaza de la Provincia in Madrid.

Sweden

464 ● Sweden. Trumpeters accompany the changing of the Swedish Royal Guards at the Royal Palace in Stockholm.

464-465 ● Sweden. The Swedish Royal Guard boasts the longest active service in the world: the regiment was formed in 1521.

Canada

466 ● Canada. Wearing red worsted jackets, lancers of the Mounted Police prepare for a Musical Ride, in which 32 officers perform complex figures on horseback to military band music.

467 ● Canada. Saddlecloths bear the monogram "MP", shorthand for the Royal Canadian Mounted Police.

Canada. Units of horseback police (the famous Mounties) exhibit their skills at the gallop in a simulated charge in formation.

India

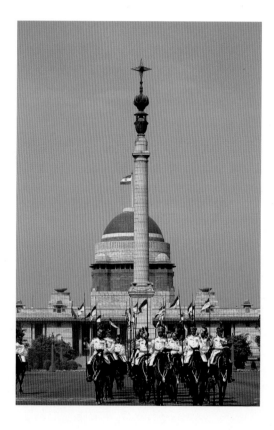

India. In New Delhi, units of the Presidential Guard maneuver in front of Rashtrapati Bhavan, the residence of the President of India.

from 472 to 475 ● India. Each year the Indian government invests large sums in the organization of the magnificent parades that celebrate the anniversary of the republic in the largest cities.

EQUESTRIAN SPORTS

PAOLO MANILI

● Great Britain. Polo requires daring, speed and skill by both horses and riders.

INTRODUCTION Equestrian Sports

IT IS THANKS TO EQUESTRIAN SPORTS THAT HORSES HAVE SURVIVED THE ADVENT OF THE COMBUSTION ENGINE. WITH THE LESSENING OF THEIR FUNCTIONS AS A MEANS OF TRANSPORT AND A WORKING ANIMAL, THEY ONLY REMAIN IN USE IN ARMIES FOR TRAINING PURPOSES AND EXHIBITIONS. IT IS FROM CAVALRY EXERCISES THAT MODERN THREE-DAY 'EVENTING' IS DERIVED (ALSO KNOWN AS HORSE TRIALS, CONCOURS COMPLET, AND MILITARY COMPETITION). IN EVENTING, A HORSE IS PUT THROUGH THREE SEPARATE TRIALS ON CONSECUTIVE DAYS: DRESSAGE IN THE RING, A CROSS-COUNTRY ENDURANCE WITH JUMPS, AND SHOW JUMPING. EVENTING IS AN INDIVID-

Switzerland. The White Turf is held each year in an unusual location for horseracing: the surface of the lake in St. Moritz.

INTRODUCTION Equestrian Sports

UAL OLYMPIC SPORT ALONG WITH DRESSAGE AND SHOW-JUMPING.

THE FORMER, WHICH HAS ITS ORIGINS IN THE RIDING SCHOOLS OF THE

17TH AND 18TH CENTURIES, IS A DEMONSTRATION OF THE HORSE'S

OBEDIENCE THROUGH A SERIES OF MOVEMENTS PERFORMED INSIDE

A RECTANGLE OF PARTICULAR SIZE. SHOW-JUMPING HAS COMPETI-

TIONS OF A DIFFERENT NATURE AND IS DERIVED FROM HUNTING: TO

PROVE THE ABILITIES OF A HORSE, THE ANIMAL WAS MADE TO JUMP

BARRIERS CONSTRUCTED TO RESEMBLE NATURAL OBSTACLES

FOUND IN THE COUNTRYSIDE. IT WAS BUT A SHORT STEP FROM THIS

TO THE ORGANIZATION OF COMPETITIONS. THE BASIS OF THE MODERN

TECHNIQUE – WHICH WAS CODIFIED AT THE START OF THE 20TH CEN-

INTRODUCTION Equestrian Sports

TURY BY CAPTAIN FEDERICO CAPRILLI OF THE ITALIAN CAVALRY AND

INITIALLY TAUGHT AT THE PINEROLO SCHOOL – SPREAD AROUND THE

WORLD. OTHER EQUESTRIAN SPECIALTIES ARE PRACTICED AT DIFFER-

ENT LEVELS IN ALMOST ALL COUNTRIES, EACH WITH ITS OWN COMPE-

TITION CALENDAR THAT INTEGRATES THE CONTINENTAL AND WORLD

CHAMPIONSHIPS. FOR EXAMPLE, ENDURANCE RACES OVER DIFFER-

ENT DISTANCES, ONE-, TWO- OR FOUR-HORSE HITCHES IN WHICH

CARRIAGES ARE PULLED BY HORSES OVER COURSES TO DEMON-

STRATE MANEUVERABILITY, AND VAULTING, IN WHICH A RIDER PER-

FORMS ARTISTIC AND GYMNASTIC MOVEMENTS WHILE THE HORSE IS

MOVING IN A CIRCLE. THE LIST IS COMPLETED BY POLO, A SPORT THAT

Equestrian Sports
Introduction

ORIGINATED IN INDIA AND THAT THE BRITISH IMPORTED TO EUROPE,

AND HORSE-BALL, WHICH IS A SORT OF FOOTBALL ON HORSEBACK.

THE OTHER HALF OF THE EQUESTRIAN UNIVERSE IS REPRESENTED BY

WESTERN RIDING, INCLUDING CONTESTS THAT SIMULATE WORK SITU-

ATIONS, LIKE ROUNDING UP CATTLE ON HORSEBACK. FROM THEIR ORI-

GIN AMONG THE NOBILITY AND ELITE, EQUESTRIAN SPORTS HAVE BE-

COME INCREASINGLY POPULAR AND WIDESPREAD, AND THUS GIVEN A

BOOST TO THE IMPROVEMENT OF HORSE-BREEDING. RIDING IS ALSO A

VERY 'MODERN' SPORT IN WHICH MEN AND WOMEN COMPETE TO-

GETHER, WITH THE LATTER OFTEN TAKING THE PRIZES.

● The Netherlands. Approaching the fence, horse and rider are in total harmony.

Showjumping

484 ● The Netherlands. At the 'top' of the jump, the horse seems suspended in the air.

485 ● Sweden. As the horse leaves the ground, the rider thrusts his weight forward
to assist his mount in the jump.

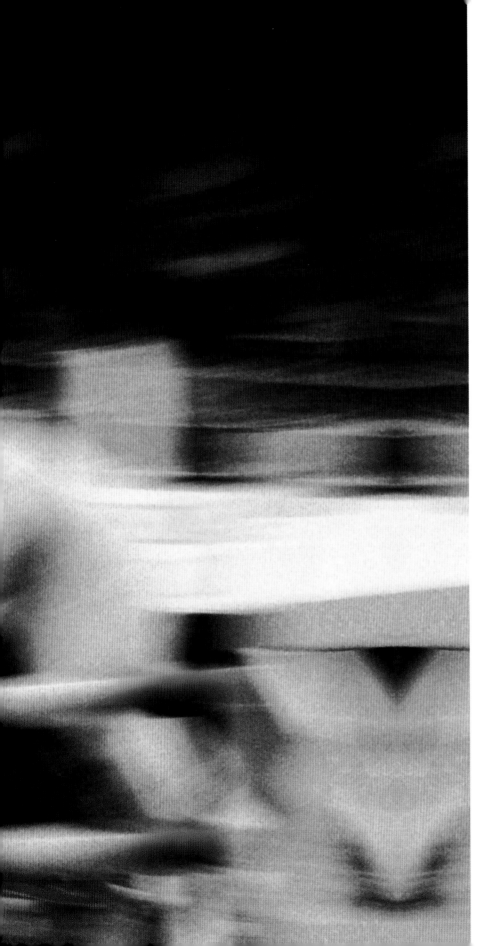

Ireland. Once the jump is under way, the rest is up to the horse; the rider can no longer use the reins or whip to guide his mount.

488 ● Ireland. Landing is the most difficult phase for the rider, and it is easy to lose balance and fall.

489 ● Ireland. A 'messy' jump; the front legs are gathered unevenly toward the chest.

● Scotland. The horse counts on its rider to manage the jump: the least uncertainty in the approach or on the rider's part and the horse refuses the jump.

from 492 to 495 ●
Spain and Great Britain.
The fall of the horse, rider
or both usually carries a
heavy penalty and, in
certain competitions,
elimination.

Dressage

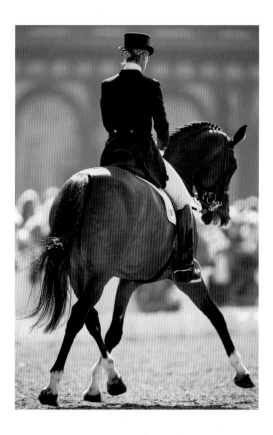

496 ● Spain. During the diagonal, the horse moves between opposite corners of the arena.

496-497 ● Spain. Elegance, balance, naturalness and perfect understanding: dressage is one of the noblest equestrian disciplines, as shown here.

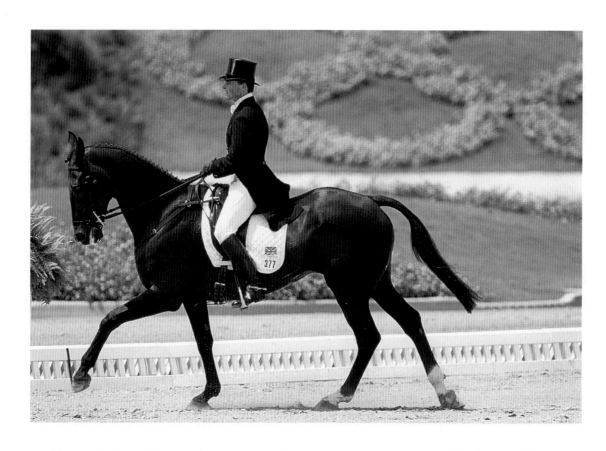

498 ● Australia. At a walking pace, the horse moves with a measured but powerful gait.

499 ● Australia. Communication between horse and rider passes through the bit: the connection between the hands of the rider and the mouth of the horse is called 'contact.'

Australia. A strong emotional bond unites rider and horse. At the end of an Olympic dressage competition, a rider compliments her horse with a caress.

● Spain. Words and physical contact
establish the fellowship required to
attempt a dressage competition.

Polo

● Switzerland. In the spectacular snow polo matches, players use a red ball, much larger
than the traditional white ball.

Switzerland. The famous Cartier Polo World Cup is held in late January on the frozen surface of the St. Moritz lake.

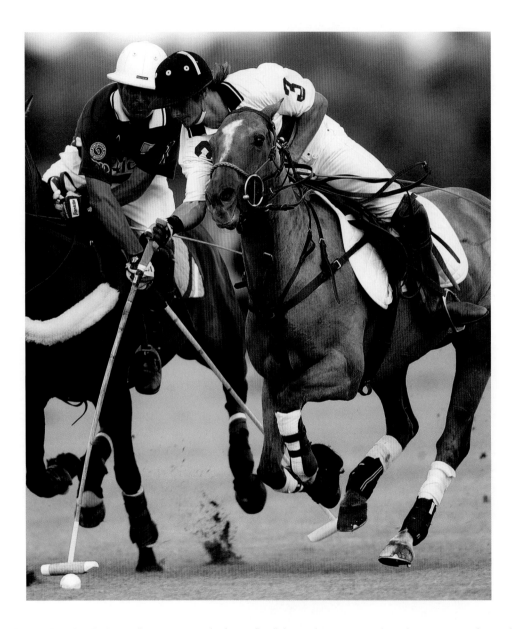

● Great Britain. Polo mallets are made from flexible malacca wood and are approximately 52 inches long.

510-511 ● USA. Polo horses have to have strong hocks to deal with the physical strain: often the animals are ponies rather than horses.

512-513 ● Great Britain. To prevent dangerous collisions in polo, complex rights govern precedence.

from 514 to 517 • USA. Given the forcefulness of the game, hocks and shins are protected by pads to prevent excessive impact, but tails are also tied up to stop them getting tangled.

Trial

● USA. The demanding Horse Trials are held over varied terrain with both artificial and natural obstacles, often with water.

Great Britain. Dramatic falls are not rare in Horse Trials.

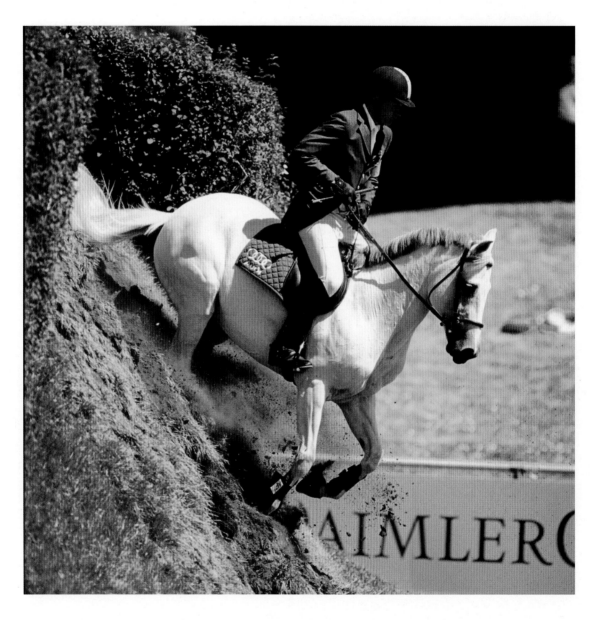

Great Britain. Dealing with embankments requires great power going up and total control of the horse coming back down.

Great Britain. Frequent falls require that the horses' legs are well protected with padding and special ointments.

Great Britain. As the pair are racing against the clock, Horse Trials are based on speed rather than style.

Harness

● Great Britain. Harness
racing includes different
categories: singles, pairs,
tandem driving (two
horses in a row) and, as
shown here, fours.

530-531 and 531 ● Great Britain.
At harnesses races there is a delightful
air of yesteryear.

532-533 ● Great Britain. In singles
driving, with a jockey and assistant,
notable speeds can be reached.

Trotting

from 534 to 541 •
Switzerland, Austria,
USA. Drivers in harness
racing or trotting races
sit in small, very light
metal gigs with rubber-
tired wheels known as
sulkies.

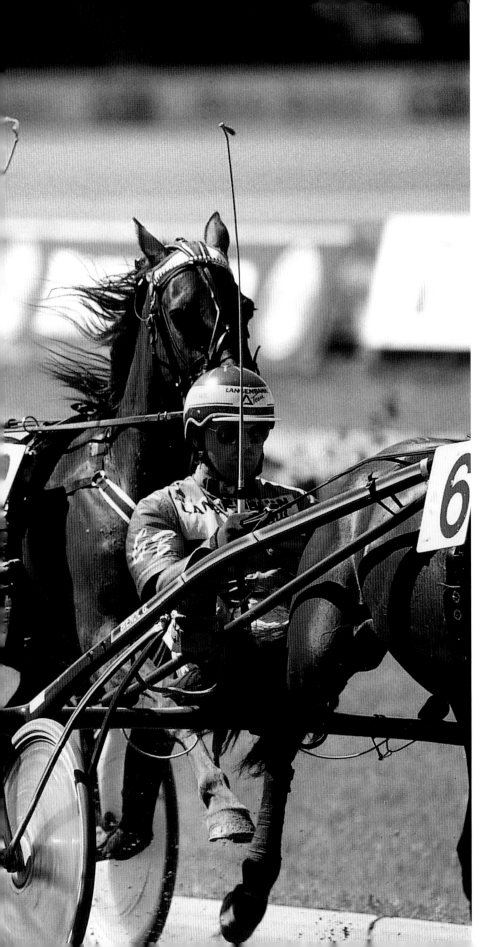

● USA. The public identify competitors in harness racing by the colors the drivers wear.

Steeplechase

from 544 to 549 ● Great Britain, Ireland. Steeplechasers require exceptional strength to tackle races over distances of 3,000 meters, jumping hedges, walls and ditches.

Great Britain, Ireland. Because steeplechase jumps cannot be moved, riders sometimes have to take 'to the air.'

Racing

from 552 to 555 ●
Switzerland. A rider at full gallop flies out of a cloud of snow. This is the White Turf in St. Moritz, a sporting event that combines international trotting and galloping races.

from 556 to 559 ● USA. Gates are needed to keep the chafing runners in line and apart. The instant they open, the horses unleash all their power in surging forward.

560-561 ● USA. Speed is not everything in a race. Depending on individual characteristics, there are 'fast' and 'slow'; horses: it is strategy not speed alone that wins races.

● USA. Similar to the blasons of medieval riders, the colors the jockeys wear identify the horses' owners.

564-565 ● Spain. Pineda race track in Seville resounds to the thunder of hooves.

566-567 ● China. Saddle and harness are reduced to the minimum so the horses carry the lightest weight possible.

568 ● Australia. This is the lead group in the Great Metropolitan Stakes in Randwick, Sydney, where races have been held since 1866.

569 ● Australia. Racehorses begin their training at the age of two. The best are soon entered in races, others begin at up to five years of age.

Great Bretain. Given the high speed on the track and flying divots of turf, jockeys wear goggles. Ventilation holes at the sides prevent the problem of fogging up.

572 ● Ireland. The Galway Races have been held since the 13th century.

572-573 ● Australia. To assist the horse's movements, the jockey leans forward, seldom in contact with the saddle.

574-575 ● Ireland. Horses exhibit their full power in the gallop.

576-577 ● USA. The public loves horseracing because of the beauty of horses at full gallop.

Canada, Great Britain. Winners: a kiss for the horse is a demonstration of gratitude and affection.

The MAJOR SCHOOLS

PAOLO MANILI

France. An instructor at the Cadre Noir School in Saumur, wearing a kepi and black uniform, directs a horse in a spectacular *cabriole*.

INTRODUCTION The Major Schools

IN *HIPPARCHIKOS* ('CAVALRY OFFICER') WRITTEN IN 362 BC, XENOPHON REFERRED TO 'SCHOOL WORK' WHICH INVESTIGATED HARMONY OF MOVEMENT IN THE GAIT OF A HORSE. RIDING METHODS TAUGHT DURING THE RENAISSANCE TENDED TO EMPHASIZE EXECUTION OF MOVEMENTS BECAUSE AT THAT TIME FIREARMS HAD MADE ARMOR OBSOLETE AND THEREFORE GREATER MANEUVERABILITY WAS REQUIRED FROM HORSES. SINCE THEN, UP TILL THE PRESENT DAY RIDING HAS EVOLVED FROM THAT DEVELOPMENT. IN THE 16TH CENTURY RIDING WAS A 'CONSTRICTIVE' ACTIVITY, AT TIMES BRUTAL (LIKE THAT OF FEDERICO GRISONE, A PUPIL OF GIOVANBATTISTA PIG-

Austria. Like a flesh-and-blood equestrian monument, a Lipizzaner performs a *courbette* at the Spanish Riding School in Vienna.

INTRODUCTION The Major Schools

NATELLI, WHO WAS MASTER OF THE RIDING SCHOOL OF NAPLES) DUE

TO THE HEAVY AND 'COLD' TYPE OF HORSES USED. HOWEVER, THE

EQUESTRIAN ARTS GRADUALLY INCREASED THE STYLIZATION OF THE

MOVEMENTS OF A HORSE IN BATTLE UNTIL THEY DEVELOPED INTO

THE REFINED MOVEMENTS TAUGHT TODAY IN RIDING SCHOOLS.

DRESSAGE WAS EXALTED IN THE HIGH SCHOOL WHICH LED, IN THE

17TH CENTURY, TO THE HIGHLY REFINED TECHNIQUES PRACTICED BY

PLUVINEL AND NEWCASTLE. FRANÇOIS ROBICHON DE LA GUERINIÈRE

(1687–1751), THE FATHER OF FRENCH EQUESTRIANISM, TOOK RIDING

TO THE FIRST, INCISIVE REVOLUTION, ONE THAT ATTEMPTED TO MEDI-

ATE RIDING VIRTUOSITY WITH PRACTICALITY IN THE USE OF A HORSE.

INTRODUCTION The Major Schools

AFTER HIM, ACADEMIC RIDING CONTINUED TO DEVELOP UNTIL THE

19TH CENTURY WHILE HISTORICAL EVENTS DEMANDED A MORE VER-

SATILE USE OF SADDLE HORSES. AT THE START OF THE 20TH CENTU-

RY, FEDERICO CAPRILLI (1868–1907), A CAPTAIN IN THE ITALIAN CAVAL-

RY, CODIFIED THE 'NATURAL SYSTEM OF RIDING,' IN WHICH THE RIDER

HAD TO ADAPT HIMSELF TO THE NATURAL BALANCES EXISTING IN THE

HORSE'S GAIT RATHER THAN VICE VERSA. THIS WAS THE SECOND AND

MORE FAR-REACHING REVOLUTION TO TAKE PLACE IN EQUESTRIAN-

ISM AND BECAME THE BASIS FOR MODERN RIDING TECHNIQUES.

TAUGHT BY THE SCHOOL OF PINEROLO AND SOON SPREAD AROUND

THE WORLD, PARTICULARLY WITH REGARD TO JUMPING, IT DIS-

The Major Schools
Introduction

PENSED WITH THE STANDARD RIDING TECHNIQUES TAUGHT. HOWEVER, SOME TRADITIONAL SCHOOLS HAVE SURVIVED TO THE PRESENT, FOR EXAMPLE THE SPANISH SCHOOL IN VIENNA (FOUNDED IN 1792 BY CHARLES V HABSBURG) AND THE SAUMUR SCHOOL IN FRANCE (FOUNDED IN THE MID-18TH CENTURY BY THE DUKE OF CHOISEUL). BOTH ARE 'SHRINES' TO HORSE RIDING AND REPRESENT AN INESTIMABLE TECHNICAL AND CULTURAL VALUE. IN ORDER THAT SPANISH TRADITIONS MIGHT BE PRESERVED, IN 1987 THE REAL ESCUELA ANDALUZA DEL ARTE EQUESTRE WAS FOUNDED IN JEREZ DE LA FRONTERA IN ANDALUSIA BY ALVARO DOMECQ ROMERO. THESE THREE ACADEMIES REPRESENT THE HISTORY OF HORSE RIDING.

● France. The name "Cadre Noir," applied to the Saumur school's officials, was later applied to the school itself. It comes from the color of the instructors' uniform.

"LEAPING HORSES THAT CREATE FLESH-AND-BLOOD EQUESTRIAN MONUMENTS, HORSES THAT BUCK AND REAR WITH A SENSE OF ART AND PROPORTION, HORSES THAT DANCE: IT TAKES DISCIPLINE TO DO ALL THIS. AT THE TEMPLES OF THE ART OF RIDING, HOWEVER, MAN AND HORSE LEARN TOGETHER, AND IT IS THE FORMER WHO MUST ADAPT TO THE LATTER."

● Spain. An enthralling sequence in a *cabriole* in four consecutive photographs: only horses with perfectly trained rear muscles are capable of this exercise.

France. In the culminating phase of the *cabriole*, the horse, which is completely off the ground, kicks vigorously backwards.

France. The *croupade* is part of the so-called *Arie Alte*, i.e., the figures in which the horse lifts all four legs at the same time.

Real Escuela Andaluza
del Arte Equestre
Jerez (Spain)

● Spain. Trainers at work at the Real
Escuela Andaluza del Arte Ecuestre in
Jerez de la Frontera: the renowned
school's pride is the exhibition of How
Andalusian Horses Dance, which leaves
no doubt as to the excellence of the art
practiced here.

596 ● Spain. The covered ring of the Picadero in Jerez de la Frontera is where the Real Escuela Andaluza del Arte Ecuestre has given its performances since 1987.

597 ● Spain. With its front legs high against its chest, a horse executes a *courbette*, a figure in which the animal makes small jumps forward balancing only on its hind legs.

Le Cadre Noir
in Saumur

France

● France. The 'career' of the Cadre Noir horses (shown here in a *croupade* and a *courbette*) lasts only about 15 years; they are then sold to other schools, breeders or private individuals.

● France. An elegant croupade at the Cadre Noir in Saumur. At the rider's command, the horse 'bucks', extending its rear legs completely.

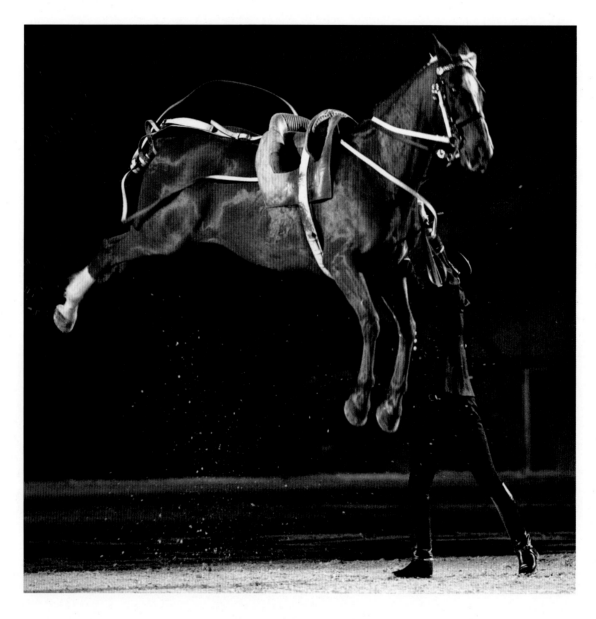

602 and 603 ● France. An instructor at the school in Saumur uses a long rein while training a horse to perform the *cabriole*.

604-605 ● France. In the Cadre Noir riding school, two groups of five horses execute a *croupade* in sequence.

Spanische
Reitschule Vienna

Austria

from 606 to 611 ● Austria. Most of the magnificent and highly trained horses at the Spanish Riding School in Vienna (Spanische Reitschule) are Lipizzaners.

HORSES on PARADE

SENIO SENSI

• New Zealand. A rodeo contestant shows skill and a sense of acrobatics
in the saddle on an untamed horse.

INTRODUCTION Horses on Parade

THE LOVE FELT FOR HORSES IS SHOWN IN MANY PARTS OF THE WORLD BY THEIR MAJOR ROLE IN OUTSTANDING NATIONAL EVENTS AND CELEBRATIONS. WHETHER IT'S PARADES AND REVIEWS, MEDIEVAL PROCESSIONS, OR RACING, CULTURAL AND RECREATIONAL EVENTS, HORSES BRING SPLENDOR AND HONOR TO THEM WITH THEIR REGAL BEARING AND ABUNDANT ENERGY. FROM THE VIOLENT TWO- AND FOUR-HORSE CHARIOT RACES THAT ROUSED AUDIENCES IN ANCIENT ROME'S CIRCUSES, TO THE "ROMANTIC" TOURNAMENTS OF THE MIDDLE AGES, IN WHICH MAGNIFICENTLY ARMORED AND CAPARISONED HORSES SHARED THE GLORY WITH DUELING KNIGHTS,

● Italy. Since 1644, the year it was first run, Siena's Palio has been a major event for the citizens.

INTRODUCTION Horses on Parade

AND FROM POLO, PLAYED IN PERSIA OVER 1,000 YEARS AGO, TO PA-

TO, A SORT OF HORSE-BORNE BASKETBALL INVENTED IN ARGENTINA

AROUND 1600, HORSES HAVE BEEN INDISPENSABLE TO MANY TYPES

OF RECREATION.

THEN THERE ARE RECENTLY INVENTED WESTERN COMPETITIONS

LIKE BARREL RACING (A RACE BASED PRIMARILY ON SPEED AROUND

A COURSE MARKED BY THREE BARRELS INSIDE A CORRAL), POLE

BENDING (LIKE AN "EQUESTRIAN SLALOM" THROUGH A COURSE

MARKED BY SEVEN POLES), AND OF COURSE THE FAMOUS AND TRA-

DITIONAL RODEOS, IN WHICH COWBOYS ATTEMPT TO RIDE WILD

HORSES.

INTRODUCTION Horses on Parade

EUROPE HAS SEVERAL EQUIVALENTS OF THE AMERICAN COWBOYS:

THE *CSIKOS*, OR HUNGARIAN STOCKMEN, WHO PERFORM AMAZING

STUNTS ON HORSEBACK AT LOCAL SHOWS AND FAIRS, THE *GARDI-*

ENS OF THE CAMARGUE, WHO ANNUALLY PARADE ON HORSEBACK

THROUGH THE STREETS OF ARLES DURING THE *FÊTE DES GARDIENS*,

AND THE ITALIAN *BUTTERI*, WHO SHOW OFF THEIR RIDING SKILLS AT

TRADITIONAL EVENTS LIKE THE MERCA IN MONTEROMANO, A FAIR

THAT FOCUSES ON CATTLE BRANDING. THEN TOO, MENTION MUST

BE MADE OF THE FAMOUS HORSE RACES ON SNOW AT ST. MORITZ IN

SWITZERLAND, INAUGURATED IN 1984 AND SOON COPIED IN SIMILAR

COMPETITIONS IN LECH (AUSTRIA) AND MÉGÈVE (FRANCE), AND THE

INTRODUCTION Horses on Parade

FANTASIES IN MOROCCO, THE MOST IMPORTANT OF WHICH IS HELD

IN HONOR OF IDRIS I (THE FATHER OF THE NATION). AS EVENING

FALLS, A MULTICOLORED CAVALRY SIMULATES A CHARGE, FIRING

LONG-BARRELED, DECORATED AND SILVER-CHASED RIFLES INTO

THE AIR. IN SPAIN HORSES TAKE PART IN LONG ESTABLISHED EVENTS:

IN SEVILLE, FOR EXAMPLE, DURING THE FERIA IN APRIL, THE CITY FILLS

WITH HORSES DECKED OUT IN FINE TRAPPINGS AND RIDERS IN THE

TRADITIONAL COSTUME OF THE ANDALUSIAN FAIR, BOTH EQUALLY

PROUD. AND IN MAY IN JEREZ THE FERIA DEL CABALLO IS THE FA-

VORITE OCCASION OF HORSE ENTHUSIASTS. THE CITY CAN ALSO

BOAST THE REAL ESCUELA ANDALUZA DE ARTE ECUESTRE DI JEREZ,

INTRODUCTION Horses on Parade

ONE OF THE MOST RENOWNED RIDING SCHOOLS IN THE WORLD. IN

ITALY THE SARTIGLIA OF ORISTANO HAS BEEN FAMOUS SINCE 1543;

THIS IS A PARADE OF CAPARISONED HORSES RIDDEN BY MASKED

HORSEMEN PERFORMING ELEGANT MANEUVERS.

BUT SURELY THE PERFECT COMBINATION OF MAN AND MOUNT

TAKES PLACE IN SIENA AT THE PALIO. THIS EVENT IS A RACE OF THREE

LAPS AROUND THE PIAZZA DEL CAMPO IN WHICH THE WINNER IS

CONSIDERED TO BE THE HORSE, NOT THE RIDER. IN FACT, THE HORSE

IS ABLE TO TAKE HIS CONTRADA (CITY QUARTER) TO VICTORY EVEN

IF HIS RIDER HAS BEEN UNSEATED.

BEFORE THE RACE THE HORSES ARE BLESSED IN CHURCH AND, IN

Horses on Parade
Introduction

THE EVENT OF VICTORY, IS SEATED AT THE HEAD OF THE TABLE DUR-

ING THE CELEBRATORY FEAST THAT FOLLOWS. WATCHED OVER

NIGHT AND DAY, THE HORSES UNLEASH THEIR NERVOUS ENERGY ON

THE PIAZZA DEL CAMPO WHERE THEIR SAFETY AND WELL-BEING ARE

GREATER THAN ANYWHERE ELSE IN THE WORLD.

WHEN THEY REACH OLD AGE, THEY ARE PENSIONED OFF IN A MEAD-

OW AND, ON THEIR DEATH, THEY OFTEN RECEIVE THE TRIBUTE OF A

TOMB AND DEATH NOTICE THAT DESCRIBES THEIR RACING

PROWESS. IF I WERE A HORSE, I WOULD WANT TO RACE IN THE PALIO

IN SIENA. AND I'M NOT THE ONLY ONE.

● Afghanistan. In a wild whirlwind of dust, a horde of riders attempts to win a goat.
This is *Buskashi,* the Afghani national sport that boasts ancient origins.

Feria de Abril

Seville - Spain

622 ● Spain. During the Fería de Abril in Seville, the bright colors of flamenco costume offset the glossy coats of the horses.

622-623 ● Spain. Man and horse become a single unit when expressing Andalusian pride.

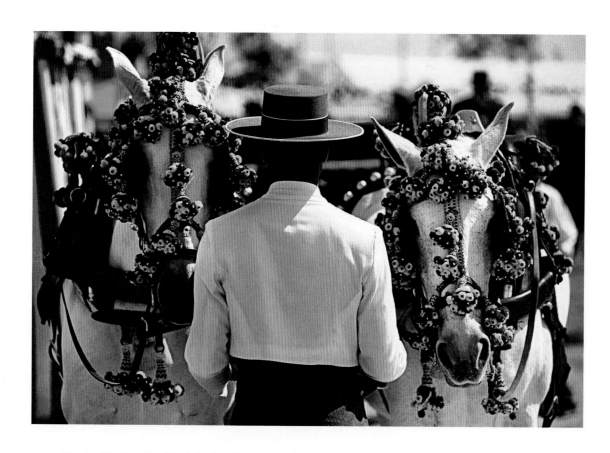

Spain. During the Fería in Seville, the horses' heads are adorned with floral ornaments.

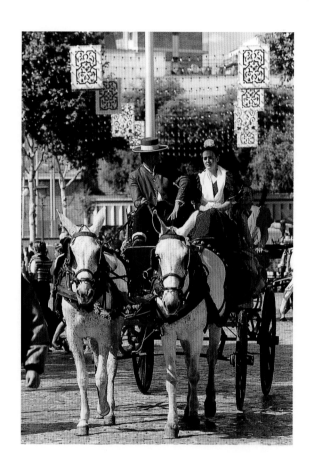

Spain. On the first day of the Fería, which begins the week after Easter, participants arrive in the city on horseback or on carts pulled by twosomes or foursomes.

from 628 to 631 ● Spain. During the Feria de Abril, the gestures, poses and garb of a romantic and not-so-distant past are revived with powerful spontaneity.

Feria de Jerez

Jerez de la Frontera, Spain

632 and 633 ● Spain. Horses' tails embellished with bright ribbons: the decorations worn by the riders blend with the beauty of the animals at the Fería in Jerez.

from 634 to 637 ● Spain. The parade of the horses and carriages in the ring is a highlight of the Fería.

Fiesta de San Juan
Minorca - Spain

● Spain. At the Fiesta di San Juan, which takes place in the streets of Minorca's old Muslim quarter, the horses move fearlessly through the crowd.

Spain. The king of the Fiesta is the Minorcan horse, appreciated for vigor coupled with ridability.

Spain. During the Fiesta, the horses change their gaits in response to their riders' orders.

Luminarias
San Bartolomé de los Pinares
Spain

● Spain. A rider faces the flames with his horse, symbolically purifying the animal during the *Festival Luminarias* at San Bartolomé de los Pinares, in the province of Avila.

Spain. The *Luminarias* festival is a religious celebration held on the night before St. Anthony's day, the patron saint of animals.

Palio di Siena

Italy

● Italy. The Palio di Siena always arouses high excitement in the riders, the horses and the public.

Italy. Conveyed back to the height of the Middle Ages in the scene in the Piazza del Campo, the electrified audience follows the horserace. The event acquires an even more spectacular air as the pounding hooves throw up enveloping clouds of ocher earth.

Italy. During the Palio, the horses absolutely maximize their strength and stamina.

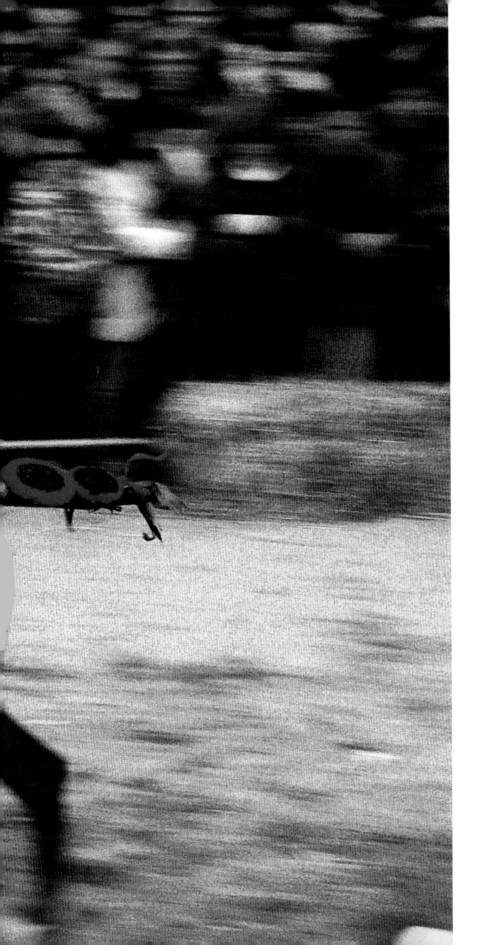

Sartiglia di Oristano
Italy

Italy. The Sartiglia di Oristano is a joust instituted in 1543 to control the bloody clashes that took place between the Arborensi and Aragonesi.

● Italy. In the *sartiglia* in Oristano (a game of Arabian-Iberian origin), riders perform a series of difficult exercises before the crowd.

● Italy. The riders in Oristano perform acrobatic tricks like the human pyramid, the 'bridge' or the 'laterali in piedi.'

Oswald von Wolkenstein Ritt

Italy

● Italy. The Ride (Ritt) of Oswald von Wolkenstein, named after the celebrated mediaeval troubadour who lived here, is an event with games on horseback. It is held every June on the Sciliar Plateau.

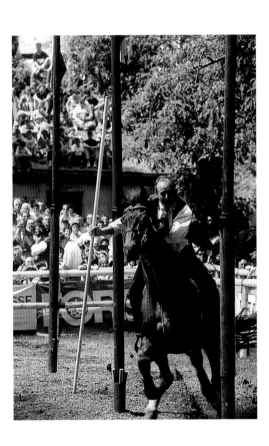

Italy. A set course includes games and tournaments that require ability, speed and precision.

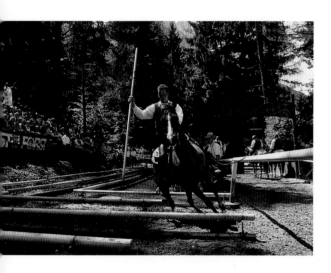

● Italy. Rider and horse must work
in perfect harmony to be able to
deal with the narrow spaces of
each obstacle.

Puzta horsemen

Hungary

from 666 to 669 ●
Hungary. During the equestrian events held on the *puszta*, the *czikos* – Magyar cowboys – show off with daredevil and dramatic acrobatics.

Ride of the Kings
Czech Republic

● Czech Republic. Once widespread throughout Moravia, today the Ride of the Kings is held only in the village of Vlcnov. During the festivities, which are part of the Easter celebrations, the horses' manes and coats are decorated with multicolor ribbons.

672-673 ● Czech Republic. A triumph of colors accompanies the King, in the center, escorted by two horsemen.

673 ● Czech Republic. Damsels dressed in the rich traditional costumes of Vlcnov participate in the Ride of the Kings.

Fantasia

Morocco

674 and 675 ● Morocco. Fantasia are ceremonial simulations of a cavalry charge, symbolized by the shots fired into the air.

from 676 to 679 ● Morocco. Fantasia is an opportunity to revive warrior traditions as well as a patriotic sense of belonging.

Durbar Festival

Nigeria

● Nigeria. The celebrations of the Durbar Festival start at the end of Ramadan. The parade features fast-paced riding, in which participants raise their lances and swords to the sky.

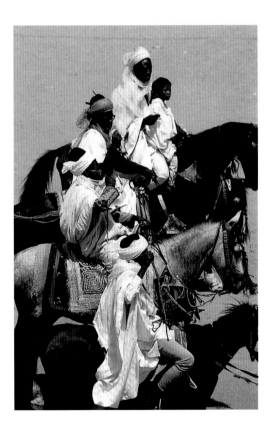

682-683 ● Nigeria. The dark faces of the men blend with the black coats of the horses, thereby emphasizing the colors of the garments.

683 ● Nigeria. Nigerian and Berber ponies, which are small, agile and docile horses, play a starring role in the Durbar Festival.

Buskashi

Afghanistan

684 and 685 ● Afghanistan. The *Buskashi* is the Afghan national sport; it is a horseback
struggle to win the body of a decapitated goat.

686-687 ● Afghanistan.
The *Buskashi* is not really
a team game. The aim is
simply to better
everybody else.

Afghanistan. Violence plays a central role in trying to get possession of the goat's carcass, or what remains of it at the end of the contest.

Litang
Festival
China

from 690 to 693 ●
China. Each year on
Litang plateau in Tibet,
thousands of people
meet to challenge one
another in tests of skill on
horseback.

● China. The participants in the Litang festival are from a tribe that was once composed of ferocious warriors. Today this legacy is manifested in a spectacular festival.

Omak Stampede
USA

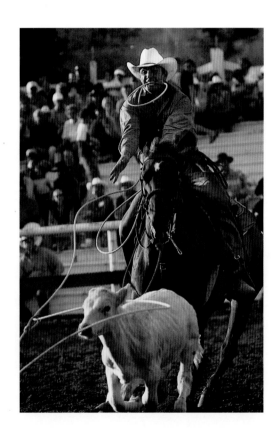

696 ● USA. A calf is immobilized with a halter during the Omak Stampede.

696-697 ● USA. A cowboy throws the lasso.

Rodeo

USA

698 ● USA. A competitor in the Cowtown Rodeo, held in New Jersey, throws himself on a bull to wrestle it to the ground.

698-699 ● USA. Having roped its horns, two cowboys win control of a young bull.

USA. A participant at the Buffalo Bill Cody Stampede Fourth of July Rodeo follows a bull on horseback.

● USA. The rodeo calls for great physical effort by horses and their riders.

Rodeo
Canada

● Canada.
As shown by the cowboy's
face, wrestling with a
young bull demands great
physical effort.

706 and 706-707 ● USA. The rodeo is not
without a violent aspect, as by the calf's
desperate flight from the mounted cowboy.

708-709 ● USA. A cowboy enters
the ring.

USA. A cowboy can barely control this bucking horse in a bronco saddle-riding competition, which consists of riding a saddled foal, or bronco.

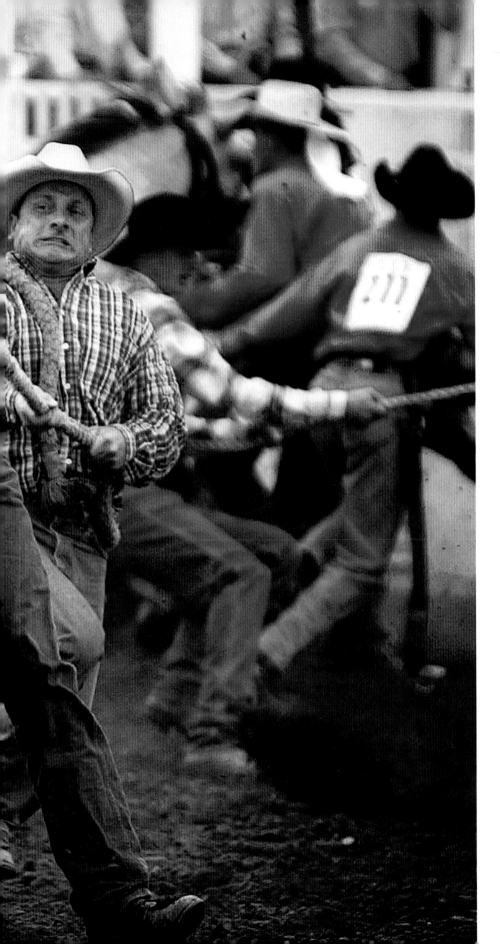

USA. During a contest, two team members attempt to control a wild horse.

714 and 715 ● USA. Remaining on a wild horse is a test that requires the utmost strength.

716-717 ● Canada. Dramatic falls are an attraction for the crowd at a rodeo.

Rodeo

Australia

- Australia. Breakaways, falls, and roll-overs are always a wild-card threat at rodeos.

Australia. The powerful ringers are accustomed to falling, but the same thing cannot be said of the untamed horses participating in rodeos. In fact, the horses are the ones that usually get hurt.

Rodeo de la Semana Criolla

Uruguay

Uruguay. During Creole week in Montevideo, Argentine, Brazilian and Uruguyuan *gauchos* challenge one another in various rodeos.

● Uruguay. Horses and *gauchos* offer acrobatic displays.

AUTHORS Biographies

GABRIELE BOISELLE

Gabriele Boiselle, who has worked professionally for many years, is one of the world's most famous equestrian photographer and her work is regularly presented in the most important horse-racing periodicals. She has also published a number of successful books.

HENRY DALLAL

Henry Dallal, who was born in Iran, is a landscape and nature photographer. His work has appeared in such publications as The Los Angeles Times, Hermes, Country Life, The Daily Telegraph, Household Cavalry Journal and Climbing. His books include *Pageantry and Performance: The Household Cavalry in a Celebration of Pictures*, the outcome of six years of work dedicated to following the Household Cavalry of Britain's Royal Guard. The results of this project have been exhibited at Windsor Castle, Kensington Palace, and the Royal Geographical Society. Dallal was also appointed to photograph H.R.H Queen Elizabeth for the cover of *All the Queen's Horses*, a tribute to Her Majesty's Jubilee. He has also contributed to *Horse Gunners: A Photographic Record of The King's Troop of the Royal Horse Artillery.*

ATTILA KORBELY

Attila Korbely is a nature photographer that has been taking pictures since his childhood. He has worked for the most important photo magazines, and published extensively on photography and ecology, becoming the most published nature photographer in Hungary. He has served as an equipment tester for Canon, as chief nature photographer for Hungary's National Geographic Magazine, and is currently president of Nimrod: The Hungarian Nature Photographers Society. Mr. Korbely has undertaken more than 10 photo expeditions in search of stories on musk oxen, deer, etc., and on the world's most endangered areas. He has spent many weeks from season to season with the Takhi horses on the Hungarian *puszta* and in the Pentezug Bioreservation, recording them from birth to death, playing, fighting, feeding, and breeding.

PAOLO MANILI

Paolo Manili was born in Milan in 1949. A professional journalist, horse expert and a member of the International Alliance of Equestrian Journalists, he was for many years an editor with Cavallo Magazine and Lo Sperone, and continues to contribute to these specialized monthlies. For ten years he wrote the equestrian and riding column for several leading Italian dailies (Il Resto del Carlino, La Nazione and Il Giorno). From 1976 to the present he has reported on the world's major equestrian events. Manili has also headed the press office for international show jumping events, including several World Cup qualifiers in Bologna and also the Milan Masters. He has collaborated with periodicals such as Capital, Gente Viaggi and Polo International. For years he handled the series of manuals for Edizioni Equestri, including Guida del Cavaliere. He also wrote the book *Graziano Mancinelli – La leggenda di un cavaliere* (Poligrafici Editoriale).

SENIO SENSI

Senio Sensi was born in Siena in 1941. As a journalist, he has collaborated with periodicals and television stations in Siena and outside the city. For eight years he was Governor of the Noble Contrada of the Goose and is currently Managing Director of the Consortium for the Protection of the Palio, in charge of Communications and Image for the Siena festival. He is co-founder and director of the magazine Il Carroccio di Siena, which discusses the city's history, culture and events.

MEDFORD TAYLOR

Medford Taylor was born in Conway, North Carolina. His passion for horses has been the hallmark of his thirty-year career. As a freelance photographer, he has worked for numerous international periodicals, including GEO, Newsweek, TIME and National Geographic Magazine. Taylor has won a number of prizes, notably awards from the Virginia News Photographers Association and the White House News Photographers Association, and he participated in international photo exhibitions, including the 1997 Visa Pour L'Image international photo festival in Perpignan, France.

INDEX

PHOTO CREDITS

PHOTO CREDITS

PHOTO CREDITS

Page 518 Gabriele Boiselle/Archiv Boiselle

Page 519 Marielle Andresson/Archiv Boiselle

Pages 520-521 Gabriele Boiselle/Archiv Boiselle

Page 521 Allsport/Inpho

Page 522 Jacques Toffi /Archiv Boiselle

Page 523 Gabriele Boiselle/Archiv Boiselle

Pages 524-525 Kit Houghton/Corbis/Contrasto

Page 526 Gabriele Boiselle/Archiv Boiselle

Page 527 Michael Crabtree/Reuters/Contrasto

Pages 528-529 Mark Barrett

Pages 530-531 Jonathan Blair/Corbis/Contrasto

Page 531 Jonathan Blair/Corbis/Contrasto

Pages 532-533 Mark Barrett

Pages 534-535 Pierre Vauthey/Corbis Sygma/Contrasto

Pages 536-537 Specht/Laif/Contrasto

Pages 538-539 Kevin Fleaming/Corbis/Contrasto

Pages 540-541 Kelly-Mooney Photography/Corbis/Contrasto

Pages 542-543 Gabriele Boiselle/Archiv Boiselle

Pages 544-545 John Walton/Empics/Contrasto

Pages 546-547 Morgan Treacy/Inpho

Pages 548-549 Patrick Bolger/Inpho

Pages 550-551 Inpho

Page 551 Lorraine O'Sullivan/Inpho

Pages 552-553 Ruben Sprich/Reuters/Contrasto

Pages 554-555 Gabriele Boiselle/Archiv Boiselle

Page 556 Mark Barrett

Page 557 Ray Stubblebine/Reuters/Contrasto

Pages 558-559 Skip Dickstein/Corbis/Contrasto

Pages 560-561 John Sommers/Reuters/Contrasto

Pages 562-563 Rick Rickman/NewSport/Corbis/Contrasto

Pages 564-565 Marcelo Del Pozo/Reuters/Contrasto

Pages 566-567 Bobby Yip/Reuters/Contrasto

Page 568 John Walton/Empics/Contrasto

Page 569 Jack Atley/Reuters/Contrasto

Pages 570-571 Mark Barrett

Page 572 Morgan Treacy/Inpho

Pages 572-573 Jack Atley/Reuters/Contrasto

Pages 574-575 Mark Barrett

Pages 576-577 Kevin R. Morris/Corbis/Contrasto

Page 578 Darren Staples/Reuters/Contrasto

Page 579 Mike Cassese/Reuters/Contrasto

Page 581 Benali-Dufour/Gamma/Contrasto

Page 583 Manfred Horvarth/Anzenberger/Contrasto

Page 587 Jacques Toffi/Archiv Boiselle

Page 588 left, center and right Gabriele Boiselle/Archiv Boiselle

Page 589 Gabriele Boiselle/Archiv Boiselle

Pages 590-591 Mark Barrett

Pages 592-593 Mark Barrett

Page 594 J.D. Dallet/Agefotostock/Marka

Pages 594-595 Corbis/Contrasto

Page 596 Nik Wheeler/Corbis/Contrasto

Page 597 Mark Barrett

Page 598 Gabriele Boiselle/Archiv Boiselle

Page 599 Gabriele Boiselle/Archiv Boiselle

Pages 600-601 Benali-Dufour/Gamma/Contrasto

Page 602 Benali-Dufour/Gamma/Contrasto

Page 603 Remi Benali/Gamma/Contrasto

Pages 604-605 Benali-Dufour/Gamma/Contrasto

Page 606 Manfred Horvarth/Anzenberger/Contrasto

Page 607 Manfred Horvarth/Anzenberger/Contrasto

Pages 608-609 Jerry Cooke/Corbis/Contrasto

Pages 610-611 Alamy Images

Page 613 Alamy Images

Page 615 Marcello Bertinetti/Archivio White Star

Page 621 Baci/Corbis/Contrasto

Page 622 Huber/Laif/Contrasto

Pages 622-623 Huber/Laif/Contrasto

Page 624 Huber/Laif/Contrasto

Page 625 Gabriele Boiselle/Archiv Boiselle

Page 626 Antonio Attini/Archivio White Star

Page 627 Antonio Attini/Archivio White Star

Page 628 Antonio Attini/Archivio White Star

Page 629 Antonio Attini/Archivio White Star

Pages 630-631 Antonio Attini/Archivio White Star

Page 632 Gabriele Boiselle/Archiv Boiselle

Page 633 Gabriele Boiselle/Archiv Boiselle

Pages 634-635 Gabriele Boiselle/Archiv Boiselle

Pages 636-637 Gabriele Boiselle/Archiv Boiselle

Pages 638 Dani Cardona/Reuters/Contrasto

Page 639 Bialobrzeski/Laif/Contrasto

Pages 640-641 Dani Cardona/Reuters/Contrasto

Page 641 Abbie Enock; Travel Ink/Corbis/Contrasto

Page 642 and 643 Huber/Laif/Contrasto

● France. Big eyes, graceful features and a prominent forehead are distinctive of the magnificent Arabian horse.